BOUND FEET & WESTERN DRESS

Pang-Mei Natasha Chang

BANTAM BOOKS
TORONTO • NEW YORK • LONDON • SYDNEY • AUCKLAND

BOUND FEET & WESTERN DRESS
A BANTAM BOOK : 0 553 50650 1

First publication in Great Britain

PRINTING HISTORY
Bantam edition published 1997
Bantam edition reprinted 1997 (twice)

Bantam Books are published by Transworld Publishers Ltd,
61–63 Uxbridge Road, London W5 5SA,
in Australia by Transworld Publishers (Australia) Pty Ltd,
15–25 Helles Avenue, Moorebank, NSW 2170,
and in New Zealand by Transworld Publishers (NZ) Ltd,
3 William Pickering Drive, Albany, Auckland.

Printed and bound in Great Britain by
Cox & Wyman Ltd, Reading, Berkshire.

AUTHOR'S NOTE

I have used the pinyin romanization system, the official romanization system of the People's Republic of China, and the one widely adopted by scholars and journalists, for the spelling of most Chinese words throughout this book. With personal names of family members and figures that are long familiar in the West, I have retained the use of the older Wade-Giles system. Thus, my great-aunt is referred to as Chang Yu-i rather than Zhang Youyi, and Chiang Kai-shek is used rather than Jiang Jieshi.

CONTENTS

CHRONOLOGY OF EVENTS

	HISTORY	CHANG YU-I	HSÜ CHIH-MO & OTHERS
1896	William McKinley elected twenty-fifth President of U.S.		Hsü Chih-mo born in Xiashi, Zhejiang province
1900	Boxer Rebellion against Europeans in China	Born in Jiading, Jiangsu province	
1902			Lu Xiaoman born
1903			Lin Huiyin born

	HISTORY	CHANG YU-I	HSÜ CHIH-MO & OTHERS
1905	Sun Yat-sen founds group of secret societies to expel Manchu rulers		Second and Fourth Brothers leave China to study in Japan until 1909
1907		Moves with family to Nanchang after "sedan chair incident"	
1910			Hsü Chih-mo attends Hangzhou Middle School until 1915
1911	Revolution against Manchu dynasty (1644–1911); Sun Yat-sen founds Kuomintang (Nationalist Party) and is elected President of the Republic one year later		
1913	Yüan Shi-kai replaces Sun Yat-sen as President	Attends Suzhou Teachers' College Preparatory School until 1915	Second Brother studies in Germany and England until 1916

	HISTORY	CHANG YU-I	HSÜ CHIH-MO & OTHERS
1914	Outbreak of World War I		
1915		Marries Hsü Chih-mo; moves to Xiashi to live in Hsü family home	
1916	Warlord era; China divided among competing warlords for next twelve years		Hsü Chih-mo attends Beijing University
1917	Revolution in Russia; Hu Shi proposes reform of Chinese language to the vernacular; Beijing government declares war on Germany		
1918	World War I ends	Gives birth to son, Hsü Chi-kai	Hsü Chih-mo travels to U.S. to study at Clark University; Second Brother studies in France and Germany until 1922

	HISTORY	CHANG YU-I	HSÜ CHIH-MO OTHERS
1919	May Fourth Movement in Beijing; U.S. President Woodrow Wilson presides over first League of Nations meeting in Paris	Begins study with private tutor	Hsü Chih-mo attends Columbia University after graduation from Clark, then abandons New York City for London
1920	Women in U.S. win right to vote	Journeys to Europe in winter to join husband	Hsü Chih-mo attends the London School of Economics; falls in love with Lin Huiyin
1921		Moves to Sawston; leaves for Paris when three months pregnant after Hsü Chih-mo's abandonment; passes pregnancy in French countryside	Hsü Chih-mo attends Cambridge University; deserts Yu-i in Sawston after asking for divorce; returns to Cambridge
1922	Mussolini forms Fascist government	Gives birth to second son, Peter, in Berlin; divorces Hsü Chih-mo; lives with Dora Berger while attending	Hsü Chih-mo divorces Yu-i in Berlin; returns to China in October; Second Brother quits Germany

HISTORY	CHANG YU-I	HSÜ CHIH-MO & OTHERS
	Pestalozzi Furberhaus to train as kindergarten teacher	and returns to China
1923		Hsü Chih-mo meets Lu Xiaoman in summer; acts as cointerpreter with Lin Huiyin on Rabindranath Tagore's tour of China; edits prestigious literary supplement of *Chenbao* (Morning Post)
1925	Sun Yat-sen dies	Peter dies at age three; Yu-i travels through Italy with Hsü Chih-mo; moves to Hamburg	Hsü Chih-mo journeys to Europe to test love for Lu Xiaoman; travels through Italy with Yu-i; returns to China
1926	Kuomintang forces led by Chiang Kai-shek embark on the Northern Expedition to wrest power from warlords	Returns to China; grants Hsü Chih-mo permission to marry Lu Xiaoman	Hsü Chih-mo marries Lu Xiaoman

	HISTORY	CHANG YU-I	HSÜ CHIH-MO & OTHERS
1927	Kuomintang forces attack Communists in Shanghai and other cities, betraying uneasy alliance formed to fight warlords	Suffers death of both parents; moves to house on Avenue Hague; teaches German at Dongwu University	Hsü Chih-mo supports himself and Lu Xiaoman by lecturing; Lin Huiyin marries Liang Sicheng
1928	Chiang Kai-shek unifies China and becomes President; Mao Zedong begins Communist guerilla movement in southeastern China; Herbert Hoover elected thirty-first President of U.S.	Begins work as vice-president of the Shanghai Women's Savings Bank and general manager of the Yunchang clothing store	Hsü Chih-mo and colleagues form book company and begin publication of literary journal, the *Crescent Moon Monthly*, the following year; Hsü Chih-mo travels to Europe via U.S.
1929	Fall of U.S. stock market		Hsü Chih-mo returns to China
1931	Japanese occupy Manchuria; establish puppet state with the last Chinese emperor, Pu Yi, as symbolic head		Hsü Chih-mo dies in airplane crash

	HISTORY	CHANG YU-I	HSÜ CHIH-MO & OTHERS
1937	Japanese occupy Shanghai; Chiang Kai-shek and Mao Zedong unite to oppose Japanese		
1941	U.S. enters World War II; Kuomintang-Communist alliance collapses		
1945	World War II ends		
1949	Mao Zedong proclaims foundation of the People's Republic of China; Chiang Kai-shek flees to Taiwan	Emigrates to Hong Kong	Most of Chang family quits China
1954		Marries Dr. Su	
1965			Pang-Mei Natasha Chang born in Boston, Massachusetts
1974		Emigrates to U.S. after death of Dr. Su	

	HISTORY	CHANG YU-I	HSÜ CHIH-MO & OTHERS
1989		Dies in New York City at age eighty-eight	

PROLOGUE

The carved mahogany trunk from China still stands in the living room of my parents' home in Connecticut, the house where I grew up. Dark and gleaming, its carved tiger-claw feet grip the ground tenaciously, holding court in a corner of the room shared by Eames and Le Corbusier. I go to the trunk, fiddling with its complicated brass fixtures, and throw back the heavy lid. There is everything in this trunk: the secrets of China, the smell of camphor and clothing, dresses of another time and place. My grandmother's embroidered silk lounging robe, my grandfather's tuxedo, white dinner jackets and jodhpurs. The aprons of my amah, Xu Ma, lovingly stitched. The cheongsams from my mother's summers in Hong Kong, slim, high-collared dresses with slits on the side. Riffling through the clothes, I know them all. Automatically, I fold and refold them, a ritual I have performed since childhood. It was my father who taught me how to fold a cheongsam, respecting the collar, the most important part of the garment. I remember feeling embarrassed that he knew so much about women's clothing, but he told me that he had learned it from his own mother as a child.

Now, I find the item I am looking for, a black cheongsam like the ones sold at Yunchang, the shop of my great-aunt, Chang Yu-i, who served as my mirror and mentor during the last years of her life. I have had this garment since I was a little child; it appeared one day amid my grandparents' things from Shanghai. The dress has no label, but Yu-i recognized it immediately as we were rummaging through the family trunk one afternoon. "This is from my store," she said, as delighted as if she had come across an old friend. From then on, I considered this dress Yu-i's and accepted its presence, as unquestioningly as I did Yu-i's gift to me during the last years of her life. It is this dress that holds us together, binds us together, transports us across the years and centuries.

Unlike most of my relatives, whom I seemed to have been born knowing, I remember distinctly the first time I met Chang Yu-i. The year was 1974. I was nine. As usual, we Changs were gathered at the Central Park West apartment of Fourth Sister. A successful clothing designer since her emigration to New York City in 1954, Fourth Sister dressed in exquisitely cut cheongsams, wore her hair up in a severe chignon, powdered her skin pale white and sported bright red lipstick.

I dreaded gatherings at her home. She would always call us, my brother, sister, and me, into the room and inquire why we were not fatter, slimmer, smarter, faster or sweeter, then laugh about us in Shanghainese as we stammered a reply. In her presence, none of us, including my mother, was allowed to wear glasses. Fourth Sister could not bear to look upon such ugliness.

The evening that I first met Yu-i, my family and I were ushered into Fourth Sister's living room. Immediately, I noticed a stranger in big bifocals sitting on the other side of the love seat from Fourth Sister. Elegant but unassuming, she seemed a complete contrast to glamorous Fourth Sister. I marveled that this stranger had been allowed to keep her glasses on.

My father announced to us children, "This is your great-auntie, Second Sister, who has just arrived from Hong Kong."

I approached Yu-i shyly. Shaking her hand solemnly, I looked past the bifocals into her eyes. There was a flicker of recognition in them as if she registered me from a place far away. I remembered feeling immediately that I could trust this woman.

She lived in an apartment on Manhattan's Upper East Side, having moved from Hong Kong only after the death of her second husband. The family referred to her as "Qing Be Be," a nickname meaning "Dearest Uncle," apparently because of a family joke that she was part man. I looked at her short hair and dark pantsuit and liked what I saw: I hated dresses and had always been called a tomboy. Though my parents never spoke of it, I had heard vague rumors from my cousins and aunts that she had been divorced. They spoke about her divorce in a way that implied scandal, sorrow. I looked into her face for signs of either and saw only calm and intelligence. But that first night I did not utter more than a few words to her. And although I saw her regularly at subsequent family gatherings, it was only about five years later that I began to speak with her.

One summer, either 1979 or 1980, my father called Yu-i and invited her to visit us for several days in Connecticut. Apparently he and Yu-i had discussed the possibility of such an outing at one of the previous family gatherings. Born in 1940, my father had known Yu-i during his childhood; he and his family had lived around the corner from her in Shanghai. When the Communists came in 1949, my father and his family moved to Hong Kong, then Tokyo, then São Paulo, Brazil, before coming to America. Yu-i left China the same year for Hong Kong, where she met her second husband and lived there until his death in 1974.

On her first visit to Connecticut, Yu-i brought with her the recipe and ingredients for *zongzi*, glutinous rice wrapped in a bamboo leaf. Under Yu-i's watchful eye, my mother and I prepared the meat and rice filling, then soaked the big bamboo leaves to soften them for wrapping. When we had produced our first finished *zongzi*, Yu-i declared our efforts a success. Each summer thereafter Yu-i brought us a new recipe: one year, for *jiaozi*, meat dumplings; another year, it was shrimp sauce. She carefully oversaw our preparations, then graded us on our achievements. I liked my great-aunt's deliberate, careful approach. As we cooked, she talked to me, half in English, half in Chinese, about the differences between China and America, and the old days versus today. I had grown up speaking English at home but began to study Chinese in high school. When Yu-i spoke to me, there was never any recrimination in her voice that I was too American or could not possibly understand the China about which she spoke. No relative from the Chang side, even my own father or grandparents, talked to me in such an easy manner.

A teenager at the time, I felt caught in the middle of an acute identity crisis. As the first generation of my family born in the States, I was torn between two cultures. Chinese-American, I longed for a country I could call my own. I wanted a future but could relate to nothing of my past. I yearned to understand my origins but felt shame about my heritage.

When I began at Harvard College in 1983, I chose to major in East Asian Studies because of the department's excellent reputation. I wanted finally to understand China. But I was baffled with systematic analyses of her political and cultural traditions. To my frustration, nothing I learned about China resonated within me, and I resented deeply suggestions from students in other majors that knowledge about China should have been "innate" for me. If I understood China no better than my classmates, most of whom were American, then what was wrong with me? Was I not Chinese enough? I often feared as much.

That year, while studying for a survey Chinese history course (widely referred to as "Rice Paddies"), I came across my family name in a few texts. The Changs were usually mentioned in connection with the May Fourth era, a period from about 1919 to 1926 that witnessed tremendous upheaval of traditional Confucian culture as Western ideals pushed to the fore. Named after the nation's first prodemocracy demonstration, which took place on Tiananmen Square on May 4, 1919, the era produced, among other contributions, a new style of written language and progressive literature. Two of my great-uncles, Chang Chia-sen and Chang Chia-ao, the ones the family called Second Brother and Fourth Brother, respectively, had been cited for their respective accomplishments in government and banking. I had known both Second Brother and Fourth Brother in my childhood. Since their deaths in the mid-1970s, I paid my respects at their grave sites on a California hillside each time I visited my father's parents in San Francisco.

And to my surprise, my great-aunt, Chang Yu-i, had also been mentioned in connection with her divorce from Hsü Chih-mo, a noted romantic poet of that time, who introduced Western forms of meter and rhyme to modern Chinese poetry and helped found an influential journal, the *Crescent Moon Monthly*. Their divorce is often referred to as the first modern divorce in China.

Returning home from college my first summer, I eagerly awaited Yu-i's visit. I had to know. Could this same woman I regarded as part respected elder and part unsophisticated immigrant be the same romantic heroine I imagined from my textbooks? A day or so after her arrival, I brought out the book with her name in it and asked her to tell me her story, from the beginning.

CHAPTER ONE

A WOMAN IS NOTHING

I am your grandfather's sister, Chang Yu-i, and before I tell you my story, I want you to remember this: in China, a woman is nothing. When she is born, she must obey her father. When she is married, she must obey her husband. And when she is widowed, she must obey her son. A woman is nothing, you see. This is the first lesson I want to give you so that you will understand.

I was born in the small village of Jiading in the Baoshan District outside Shanghai. There were twelve children in my family— eight boys and four girls—but my mama, your great-grandmother, always told people she had eight children because only the sons counted. Sons would carry forth the family name, while daughters would marry and take on the duties of their husbands' families.

When a boy was born to the house, the servants saved his umbilical cord in a jar under Mama's bed. When a girl was born, the servants buried her umbilical cord outside the house. A girl left her father's house as soon as she came of age, and there was no need to save the umbilical cord of a guest.

Your grandfather and I are brother and sister, and we are very close in age. I was born in 1900. He was born in 1902. There was another brother, Seventh Brother, who was born between the two of us. He came out only eleven months after me. There were so many little children around that I wasn't weaned until I was six years old. I could walk over to my wet amah and reach for her breasts whenever I wanted a drink. I had natural milk for so long that I never get sick, even now that I am old. I always believe this is what has made me so strong.

The family says that I was born this way, though, tough like a man. Seventh Brother, the one born only eleven months after me, was exactly the opposite. Seventh Brother was soft and weak like a woman. I took all the man out of Mama when I was born, and left Seventh Brother with only the female, the family says. That makes me laugh, but I am not sure I agree. I think what happened is that life made me hard. Think of it: at your age, eighteen, I had already been married for three years. Married at fifteen and divorced by age twenty-two. So young to go through so much.

I live on my own now in New York City—my son and grandchildren near, but not with me—which is the American way. Back in Jiading, our whole family lived together in one compound in the Chinese way. The compound stood near the center of town and had two courtyards—one formal and the other informal—and a front hall that spanned eight mahogany doors. Most homes had only a single courtyard and one hall with a front door of four, but we owned a lot of land in the area and your great-great-grandfather, my grandfather, had been a high-ranking judge of the imperial government. I never knew Grandfather Chang, but his portrait hung above the ancestral altar in the front hall that we used for guests, and a special shed in the front courtyard housed the two sedan chairs which had been presented to him by an official of the court. No family ever owned its own sedan chairs, and these were prized possessions we used only on special occasions. There came to be an unlucky story connected with these sedan chairs, but I will tell you that later. Otherwise, the natural position of the house, the *fengshui*, which, translated literally, means "wind and water," was excellent, full of good omen. From the north come winds and the enemy; from the south come sunshine and good fortune. Our compound stood on the north-south axis line facing the south, its back toward the north. We were very lucky to have found a house with this position.

My father, Baba, had two older brothers, and we lived with their families and Grandmother Chang in the rear hall off the back courtyard. Three generations living together: there were so many of us, we kept separate kitchens and servant staffs in the back of the compound. We even had one servant who just made shoes for the family. At that time, everyone wore cloth shoes, and our big family needed new shoes every day. There was also a German shepherd at the house. One of the elder cousins who studied in the West at the turn of the century had brought him home as a puppy, and he was our pet before we had to kill him. The servants did not know how to take care of that dog; they fed him so many table scraps, all his hair fell out, and he began to bleed and blister until we gave him poison so that he would die in his sleep.

Baba, my father, your great-grandfather, was a doctor, a very good one. Even today, there are people who come up to me and say, "Your father saved my mother's life," or something of that kind. Baba could heal anyone, it seemed, but the donation box he kept outside his office in the middle of town was rarely filled with money. This was because his patients did not think that money showed enough respect or gratitude. Instead, they offered him slaughtered chickens or ducks fed daily on sweet wine and rice, fresh eggs or vegetables, and sometimes even paintings. Do you know all those Chinese paintings your father has hanging in your house in Connecticut? Those came from Baba, your great-grandfather, many of them originally from Baba's grateful patients. That was how good a doctor Baba was, that he received paintings as payment. Everyone in the area knew of his collection and wanted to add to it.

All the paintings were kept in a tall mahogany cabinet in Baba's bedroom. When Baba took them out, usually only one or two scrolls at a time, he spread them on a long, low table with rounded edges made especially for viewing the works. Chinese paintings required admiration from above, Baba said, explaining that the perspective of Chinese paintings differed from Western ones. The best paintings were only hung when your grandfather, Eighth Brother, and I cleaned them, passing tiny feather dusters over the surface of the rice paper. Of all the children, your grandfather and I were the two that Baba allowed near his paintings, and he would hover behind us as we worked, explaining the genius behind a misty mountain landscape or historical portrait. Our favorite story was of Zhang Sengyao, an artist of ancient time who specialized in painting the dragon but would never fill in the dragon's eyes. One day, as Zhang Sengyao completed a magnificent dragon painting, the Emperor commanded him by imperial edict to finish the brushstrokes on the creature's eyes. Having no choice, the artist obeyed, and lo and behold, the dragon lifted his heavy wings and flew off the paper!

You must understand how I had to act in front of Baba. It was very formal. When I visit your house in the summer, I see how you act with your parents, very loose and casual, but this is not how I was taught to behave as a child. I was taught to respect my elders and behave.

The first lesson of filial piety is this: that your life and body are gifts to you from your parents. This means that it is unfilial to try to commit suicide. I tell you this now so you will understand why later, when my life was very sad, I could not kill myself. I had to honor my family and stand on my own two feet.

The second lesson is: you must always inform your parents where you are going and what you are doing. You must get their permission on important decisions in your life. Again, I tell you this so you will understand how later, when I divorced without telling my parents, I broke this rule of my past.

But the other lessons of filial piety I learned as a girl—twenty-four classical examples in all—will probably make you laugh. There was the perfect filial child who would lie in his parents' bed to warm it for them in the wintertime, and to allow the mosquitoes to feast their fill on him first in the summertime. Then there was the filial child who, on his fiftieth birthday, dressed up in baby clothes and danced for his parents so they might feel light and youthful. I liked most the story about the filial child whose sick mother longed for soup with bamboo shoots in the dead of winter. The filial child wept so heavily and sincerely onto a bamboo plantation that his tears became the soft rains of spring, and bamboo shoots burst forth through the snow for him.

This was how I was brought up, to honor and respect my family and elders. So I never entered Baba's presence unless asked, and I never left it without his telling me I could. Unless he spoke to me first, I did not speak in his presence. When he scolded me, I bowed my head in thanks for his corrections. And I never addressed my father by "you." I never said to him, for instance, "Would you like another cup of tea?" I had to say, "Baba, would Baba like another cup of tea?" Most of the time, though, I never even asked Baba about refilling his teacup; I just did it. Anticipating his wishes was even more filial.

Baba was a very fussy man with a violent temper, like your grandfather's. In fact, of all my brothers, your grandfather most resembled Baba, the same round face and high cheekbones, the same manner of raising his voice or throwing things across the room when angry. Terrible, such a temper.

Baba was extremely fussy about his food. He kept a separate kitchen, cook and kitchen staff from the rest of the extended family. Grandmother Chang, the two uncles and their families usually combined their two kitchens and staffs, while we had the other to ourselves because of Baba. In the mornings as Baba ate breakfast, Cook, First Kitchen Boy and Second Kitchen Boy would line up in front of him to announce the freshest vegetables and meats they had procured from the open market early that morning. Baba would then make the great decision about what the family would eat for lunch that day. Or sometimes, without listening to Cook, he would simply proclaim his desire. Mama said food was the only reason Baba rose from bed in the mornings, and it was true; thinking about eating and eating made Baba very happy. When he talked about food, the eyes in his narrow face fairly danced, and he was not always so short in temper. Stroking the ends of his mustache, or folding his hands across his long thin frame—he was not fat at all—he would tell Cook exactly how he wanted it done: how he wanted it to look on the serving dish, weigh on the tips of his chopsticks, roll on his tongue, sound as he chewed, feel as he swallowed, and, of course, taste as he feasted. Taste was everything. Sometimes Baba himself would go into the kitchen to oversee Cook's preparations. Most of the time, however, Baba had Mama supervise Cook, and even this was unusual for Chinese families. None of the uncles' wives ever entered their kitchens, and they would sometimes tease Mama for spending so much time in the back with the servants. But Baba was so fussy about his food, he did not care that his wife might appear improper. Also, Mama did not complain. She said if Baba wanted her in the kitchen she must obey.

Mama was only two years old when she was promised to Baba's family for marriage. Baba had not even been born yet, but their families were good friends, and it was decided among the elders that if Baba were a boy he would marry Mama. There is a famous Chinese saying: "If the wife is two years older, then the rice will be everywhere." And this was true with our family. We were very happy, and food was plentiful.

I have two names, "Yu-i" and "Chia-fen." "Chia-fen" is my formal name. The character "Chia" is very complicated to write while the character "Fen" is very simple to write. "Chia" is the generation name; all my brothers, sisters, and cousins have the character "Chia" as the first part of their name. "Chia" means fine, excellent.

Shortly after he married Mama, Baba composed a couplet for the Chang family: *chia kuo pang ming.* This means fine kingdom, bright country, and was meant to express Baba's deep love for and loyalty to China.

Each character in the poem is selected as a generation name. My generation is all named with the character "Chia." Everyone in your father's generation is named with the character "Kuo," meaning kingdom. Your generation is all named with the character "Pang," for state. Your, or rather your brother's, children's names will have the character "Ming," which means brightness. Each new generation takes the next character in the poem until we finish and then begin again.

Because the first part of the name is already given, it is very important to choose the character for the second part of the name correctly. My parents chose the character "Pao" for First Brother, the eldest child, because this meant protection, guardian, a type of security. First Brother had many responsibilities; he owned a cotton factory and was always busy supervising. Second Brother was more of a scholar—he was always reading or deep in debate with his friends—and his name, "Sen," which means majestic and dignified, suited him well. Fourth Brother's was "Ao," which was an ancient musical instrument.

My own name is "Fen," meaning "jade," which the Chinese consider fine and expensive. Jade is supposed to represent all that is perfect in human virtue. There are nine types of jade, each with different Chinese characters. My name means not the popular green "bi" jade, but the unusual, clear "fen" jade. Once, when Baba returned home from a trip, he had with him a pin that caught the sunlight and shimmered in his hand. It was a pin of "fen" jade just for me—not for any of my sisters—because of my name.

Chia-fen is my formal name. My informal name is Yu-i. This is the name I use every day. "Yu" means goodness, and "I" means propriety, righteousness. I do not know whether it is because of my name, but I have always tried to do right, first for my own family and then for my husband's family. As a result, I sometimes feel I have had no life of my own.

In 1900, the year I was born, a group of Chinese called the Boxers tried to lay siege to Western delegations in the nation's capital of Beijing. They succeeded for two days and then were slaughtered by an international army of 20,000 made up of American, Japanese and Russian forces sent in to protect their nations' holdings. Second Brother, Chang Chia-sen, who was fourteen at the time, carved up a melon from the front courtyard to explain this horrible massacre to me. The front courtyard was reserved for guests, but melons grew wild along a vine in the corner near the wall, so this is where we sat one afternoon when Second Brother said that I was old enough to understand the world around me.

Along with Fourth Brother, Second Brother was my favorite. He was clever, although absent-minded and dreamy; Fourth Brother, Chang Chia-ao, who was three years younger, acted much more deliberate and levelheaded. These two became the most famous of my brothers; after study in Japan, they returned to China to lead distinguished careers, Fourth Brother as chairman of the Bank of China and Second Brother as an influential statesman and philosopher.

In their own manner, both cared for me throughout my life. Second Brother always explained to me that which I could never learn on my own. Fourth Brother chose my scholar husband for me and instructed me how to behave correctly in public during different times of my life. He was concerned with how I was regarded from the outside. But Second Brother, unlike anybody else in my family, taught me to respect how I felt inside, no matter what showed on the outside.

That afternoon in the front courtyard, Second Brother said for me to imagine that China was the melon. We had chosen one big, firm, pale green fruit from among the others, and he passed it to me now so that I could feel its full weight heavy and ripe in my arms. Second Brother then took the melon from me and thrust a knife through the smooth skin to divide the fruit almost in half. Breaking away the bigger part of the melon, and holding it up so that its juice dripped down the back of his hand, he said, "This piece is the provinces and ports of China that the foreigners now own."

Indochina lost to France, Burma and Hong Kong to Great Britain, Manchuria and Port Arthur to Russia, Korea to Japan, Second Brother explained, scooping away the pulp of the melon half with the back of his knife. He cut me a thick slice as he named the five main ports that had been forced open to free British trade:

Amoy, Canton, Fuzhou, Ningbo and Shanghai. In nearby Shanghai, where foreign rule was the worst, foreigners governed large sections of the city with their own laws and ways, making huge profits at the expense of the Chinese people.

The Boxers were Chinese mainly from the countryside who hated all Western people and ideas and wanted to eradicate any trace of foreign thinking from China. The Qing government, which had lost a large part of China to the foreigners, hated the Westerners too. But the Empress Dowager and her court had been too slow to modernize and were too weak to act on their own. So they secretly supported the Boxers, funding battle training in the remote countryside and the movement's migration to the capital. This was where the sad part about old-fashioned thinking came in, Second Brother said. Antiforeign to the core, the Boxers believed that ancient exercises and control of breath made them invincible to bullets. Even though there had been almost as many Boxers as foreigners, the Boxers had tried to fight the international forces with lances and swords instead of firearms. Their defeat was so great, two leading Chinese officials committed suicide in humiliation. The Empress Dowager fled to the west of China disguised in coarse peasant's clothes to reestablish the imperial court in Xi'an.

All this happened the year I was born, Second Brother said, explaining something which I had felt in my heart from my beginnings but could not articulate on my own. You see, when Mama said women were nothing and my amah cursed me as a "guest" and a "wasted bowl of rice," part of me heard but part of me did not. I was born into changing times and had two faces, one that heard talk of the old and the other that listened for talk of the new, the part of me that stayed East and the other that looked West, the spirit in me that was woman and the other that was man.

CHAPTER TWO

LOTUS PETALS

I am named Pang-Mei after Chinese characters from my father's side of the family and Natasha after a character in *War and Peace* which my mother started doggedly reading before my birth because I was two weeks late. Pang means "country," and Mei means "plum blossom," the national flower of China. My father told me about the line of Changs who took their name from the family's ancestral poem, but Natasha is the name I identified most with while growing up. I loved writing it, the rise of the big N nestled against three little a's. "Natasha" was easy to pronounce, too. Only my family called me "Pang-Mei"; whenever my friends heard the name, they laughed.

I spoke English at home with my parents, and watched "The Brady Bunch" and "The Partridge Family" regularly, religiously. Playing Monkey in the Middle, Bring Home the Bacon and kickball at recess, I believed myself as American as the other kids at school, mainly white, middle-class Irish Catholics and Italians. I always knew just what to order at the ice cream stores in the mall near our house: coffee or mint chocolate chip with jimmies from Friendly's, and rocky road or jamoca almond fudge in a cup at Baskin-Robbins.

On occasion, when I walked back to the car, ice cream in one hand and the change for my mother in the other, I would hear them. Jeers from the teenagers hanging out on the corner. Chink. China-man. Ching chang chong.

Whenever something like that happened, I just wanted to dis-appear from the town where I grew up. On these afternoons, when I was reminded that I wore my difference on my face, I would hide inside our house, a green split-level set on a hill high above the street. There I could perch at the edge of the picture window in our living room and watch the other kids like ants or beetles, scurrying below.

Once, in a dressing room with my mother and sister at the shopping mall, my sister put on a dress and said in dismay, "Oh, no, not this one. It looks too Chinky." My mother's hand flew up as if to hit her—and my mother never hit us—she was so shocked. She turned to my sister with a deeply wounded look on her face and said to her, "Don't you *ever* say anything like that again."

But I understood what my sister felt. I did not want to be Chi-nese either.

Both my father, a professor, and my mother, an educator, had attended school in America since their early teens. They considered Chinese their second language. Young and handsome, they did not look like other Chinese I saw in town, laundry and restaurant peo-ple with their stooped shoulders, shuffling gaits and bad teeth that showed when they spoke. Whenever my friends first met my par-ents, they invariably commented afterward in surprise, "They don't seem Chinese," or "They don't have an accent." Back then, this made me proud.

On the other side of our driveway, in a natural sandpit as yet un-touched by my parents' landscaping efforts, my brother, sister and I built huge moundlike castles surrounded by ornate moat and irrigation systems. Or we helped my father plant spreading junipers and yew trees at the borders of our property. These were the times when we would hack at the unyielding New England soil around our house and search for China. That was what I had heard at school, that we could take a slow boat there or dig down to the other side of the earth. As much as I questioned the truth of those tales, I always heard them at the back of my head, and I used to envision how we would pull back an enormous boulder and uncover a crowded street in the middle of Beijing complete with rickshaw carriers and men in funny hats.

What always worried me was what they would do then, those Chinese. What would they do when they saw my big face staring down at them from a hole in the sky?

You ask me about my childhood. In China there is a legend that says that the moon used to be inhabited by two sisters. Their brother lived in the sun. The sisters, who were very beautiful, became embarrassed because people gazed at them so much during the night. They asked their brother to change homes with them. He laughed and told them that there were many more people about in the daytime than at night, so that even more eyes would be turned upward toward them. The sisters assured him that they had a plan to prevent people from looking at them. So they changed places. The two sisters went to live in the sun and their brother in the moon. Now, if a person tries to look at the sisters, the two women immediately prick at his eyes with their seventy-two embroidery needles which are the sun's rays.

That is the full legend, but there are many versions. Sometimes the tale is told as if the sisters never leave the moon, and other times the story is told as if the sisters' only home is in the sun. These are the versions of the story I heard from my amah and my mama when I was little. My amah, who had grown up in the country and worked in the fields as a young girl, showed me the sisters in the moon and made me marvel at the beauty of their flowing silk robes and tiny embroidered slippers. Mama, who changed my life with one brave decision when I was three years old, taught me to imagine the sisters in the sun and to trust in the truth of things beyond sight.

My vision of the sky was filled with both pairs of sisters. At night, when my amah undressed me and combed out the braids she had plaited for me in the morning, I looked out my window for the moon sisters and fell asleep with the comfort that they were there. Playing in the back courtyard during the day, I felt a glowlike heat at the top of my head and middle of my back and knew that the sisters in the sun were watching over me too. Because I had heard the two parts of the story separately as a child, both sides entered my heart; I saw the sisters in the sun, and I saw them in the moon.

On the twenty-third day of the twelfth lunar month of my third year, six days before the New Year Festival, my family celebrated the Little New Year called the Festival of the Kitchen God. We were not country folk but observed this custom for the servants who believed in the folklore of the gods. During the year we hung the image of the Kitchen God above the cooking stove in the kitchen, lit incense and provided fresh fruit for him every day. On the day of the festival, the Kitchen God ascended to the heavens to note for the Supreme God the virtues and vices of the household he governed. To ensure a favorable report from the Kitchen God, the servants prepared a feast in his honor and placed especially sticky glutinous rice dumplings on the shrine before his image so his lips would remain closed upon reaching the heavens.

Because these dumplings, filled with red bean paste, are mushy and tender, they are also supposed to soften the feet of little girls. It was the custom when I was little for a woman to have tiny, tiny feet. Westerners call them bound feet, but we call them something so much prettier in China: new moon or lotus petals, after the Tang Dynasty concubine who started the tradition. So beautiful a dancer was she that the Emperor had a larger-than-life lotus complete with pond constructed for her of metal and jewels, and, for his entertainment, asked her to wrap her feet in strips of silk cloth and dance among the petals of the lotus. Her graceful dance steps were like the new moon flitting among the clouds in the reflection of a lotus pond. The Emperor was so impressed that other women began to wrap their feet and bend their arches in the crescent shape of the new moon. That is how the tradition began.

How small, how beautiful, then, the bound foot. Give me your hand so you might see how it is done, how the toes of the feet are taught to curve gently around the sole of the foot until they touch your heel. Imagine your palm as the sole and your fingers as the toes. See how your fingers in your palm make a loose fist in the shape of a new moon? That is the bound foot—you end up walking on your heels and the knuckles of your toes—and if it is perfectly formed, you can slide three fingers into the niche between the toes and the heels.

My mother had three-inch feet that she had wrapped in fresh bandages every morning and bathed in perfumed water in the evening. When she walked, stiff-legged and sway-hipped, the tips of her embroidered slippers peeped out, first one and then the other, from the edge of her robe. My amah, who came from the countryside and whose feet were big like a man's, said if I was good I would grow up to be like my mother, pale and beautiful like one of the sisters in the moon. I had first seen these sisters at Moon Festival, the harvest celebration on the fifteenth day of the eighth month of the year, when the family ate round-layered pastries called mooncakes and pomegranates, which were in season. We then rose in the middle of the night to gather in the back courtyard, shivering in our nightclothes, and admire the harvest moon hanging full and heavy above us. I was two when my amah first bundled me in blankets in her arms and took me outside for the evening festivities. She told me to watch closely, to observe the swirl of mist around the moon and the faint craters in its surface. These were the signs of the sisters, she said, a hush of wonder in her voice. Then I saw them floating above me in the moon: two women in long lustrous robes and tiny silk slippers. Closing my eyes later that night, I still felt the luminous glare of the moon like a bright star in my head, and the two sisters drifted above me in my dreams.

On my third Festival of the Kitchen God, when I was three, my amah instructed me to eat an entire glutinous rice dumpling by myself. She said that it would help to soften me, but I did not know what she meant until the next morning. Mama and my amah arrived at my bedside with a basin of warm water and strips of heavy white cotton. They soaked my feet in the water and then proceeded to bind them with the thick wet bandages. When the bandages completed their first tight wraps around my feet, I saw red in front of my eyes and could not breathe. It felt as if my feet had shrunk into tiny insects. I began shrieking with pain; I thought I would die.

"What are you crying for?" my amah scolded me. "Every little girl wants to have her feet bound."

Mama said I would grow used to it, that there was nothing she could do. To keep me occupied, she set up a little chair in the kitchen so that I could spend the day watching the cook prepare the meals. Only the day before, I had taken it all for granted, run across this very floor. That day, my screams filled the household as long as my strength permitted. Before lunch, my father and brothers had come by to comfort me, but as the afternoon progressed only Mama and my amah appeared in the kitchen to calm me. I could not be silenced. I watched Cook's cleaver glint up and down, heard the chicken's bones crunch beneath his blows and shrieked at the sound of it. It was as if my own toes were breaking as they curved beneath my soles.

Bound feet take years of wrapping. The toe bones have to be broken slowly, carefully. Even after a young girl's feet are perfectly formed, she has to keep them wrapped so they will stay in that shape. Prospective in-laws ask: "Did she complain much during her foot-binding years?" If yes, then they would think twice. She was a complainer, then, not obedient enough. Even at age three, I knew. If I was good, Mama and Baba would say that my feet were perfectly formed golden lilies, that I had been even-tempered and docile during those difficult years. But if this were not true, everyone would know. The Kitchen God would tell the Supreme God. The matchmaker would warn prospective families. The servants would gossip about me to other servants in the town. Everyone in Jiading knew the Chang family. If I was bad, no one would want me. I would not marry and would become a disgrace to my family. And still, I cried.

For three days I sat before my amah and Mama, enduring the ritual: the removal of bloody bandages, the soaking, the rewrapping and tightening. But on the fourth morning something miraculous happened. Second Brother, who could no longer bear my screams, told Mama to stop hurting me.

"Take the bandages off," he said to Mama. "It is too painful for her."

"If I weaken now," Mama said, "Yu-i will suffer in the end. Who will marry her with big feet?"

Second Brother said that foot binding was a custom that was no longer beautiful.

Mama asked Second Brother again who would marry me if she let my feet alone. Second Brother then said: "I will take care of Yu-i if no one marries her."

Second Brother was only fifteen at the time, but he had been raised to be true to his word, and Mama relented. She called my amah over to help undo the bindings, and from that day forth I never had my feet bound again.

Shen jing bing. Crazy, my amah said about Mama's decision. Even a few years later, when the Empress Dowager passed a series of reforms banning foot binding, and Mama allowed my two younger sisters to grow their feet, my amah worried for our future. Who would marry us with big feet? We were *bu san, bu si*, neither three nor four. We could not work in the fields all day long and do the chores of a man. But neither could we just sit still and stay quiet like ladies in the female quarters.

Flat and soundless, my feet became my talisman, guiding me through a new, large, open world. In the kitchen I followed the cook around from chopping block to stove and stood easily while peeling shrimp or performing other chores; Mama sat in a chair far from the fires and wearily gave orders. The power of my feet shielded me from the jibes of my cousins; when they called me "little peasant girl," I teased them back and ran away as fast as I could. Stalking hard-shelled beetles in the back courtyard, I crushed them beneath my heel if they tried to escape.

When I was twelve, Mama gave birth to the twelfth and last child, Fourth Sister. Mama fainted during the delivery, and Baba, who was the doctor, thought we were going to lose both her and the child. He called Seventh and Eighth Brothers upstairs to Mama's room and had the two of them urinate into a bowl, which he then passed directly under Mama's nose. Young boys' urine is strong like ammonia, and Mama woke up. But we were all scared, and Mama remained weak during Fourth Sister's early years, so I was the one who chewed up rice for the baby to eat and took her out to play so that Mama could rest quietly in the house.

One day, as I was playing with Fourth Sister in the back courtyard, I dropped her hard on the ground. Stunned, she burst out crying after a few seconds. My father, who happened to see her fall, immediately came running from the house. He scooped up Fourth Sister, then hit me hard across my face and said that I had to be more careful, that I ran around wild like a country girl.

It was the only time in my life that my father ever hit me, and I stayed in the courtyard, crying, long after Baba had returned to the house with Fourth Sister. Later that afternoon Mama, who was still weak and almost never dirtied the soles of her slippers, came out of the house to sit beside me. Wiping away my tears with her hand, she held me close and said that it was hard to be as free as the sisters in the sky. No man could see them, Mama said, looking up at the sun with her half-closed eyes, but the sisters were there, dancing and playing happily in their new home.

CHAPTER THREE

FORTUNE, RANK, LONGEVITY, HAPPINESS

M y own amah came from the countryside like Yu-i's, and I loved her as I did my own mother. Xu Ma had been hired by my father's family in Shanghai during the 1930s and raised my father as a boy. Now she lived with us in the downstairs room of our house in Hamden. She was the cause for the amalgam of languages we spoke in our house: Shanghainese dialect between Xu Ma and us; English among all of us except Xu Ma; and Mandarin dialect between my mother and Xu Ma, because my mother does not speak Shanghainese.

Each morning Xu Ma dressed in the same type of clothes she had worn since her childhood in the countryside of Shanghai: a high-collared smock with asymmetrical frog enclosures, cropped dark pants, flat black slippers and often an apron which she pulled up to cover her face when she laughed very hard. Crying at letters from her son who was several years older than my father and still lived in their tiny village outside Shanghai, Xu Ma was much quieter, wiping at the corners of her eyes with the apron. I hated seeing those letters in the mailbox, the telltale red, white and blue markings of the air mail envelope. That meant that Xu Ma, red-eyed, would retire directly after dinner. She would not come into our rooms late at night to tell us stories or to pound on our backs with her open palms, counting from one to four in Shanghainese: "*Ye ni san si! Ye ni san si!*"

Whenever Xu Ma cried, it made me feel sad inside, because I knew she had lived a very difficult life. My father said that Xu Ma had been born in the outskirts of Shanghai in the early 1900s and sold when she was about eight to another poor country family who raised her as a daughter/servant alongside their son until both came of age to marry each other. This was how families who could not afford bride money for a son ensured that he would marry an obedient daughter-in-law to produce sons and to continue the family name. Xu Ma's husband grew up to be a gambler, a good-for-nothing drunk. They had their first child when she was eighteen, a son. Others followed, but Xu Ma aborted them with the young twigs of a mulberry tree stripped of bark. Two of these pregnancies were actually brought to term, but since they were females, Xu Ma pushed them down the outhouse hole to drown. She who tended the fields, cooked for her mother-in-law, cleaned the house and struggled to earn extra cash as a salt smuggler did not have time for girls.

In China during the 1920s and '30s, the exchange of salt between the provinces was regulated by the warlord of each province. Enterprising peasants like Xu Ma attempted to capture profit on the sale of salt by smuggling it between various provinces. Xu Ma would sew blocks of salt into the lining of an inner vest and layer clothes on top of the vest to appear as a fat woman. If she was caught, the provincial police or warlord guards beat her severely and then rubbed salt into her open wounds to teach her a lesson.

"Come look, *non ke ve*," she would say to me in Shanghainese whenever I was feeling particularly sorry for myself. "Come look and see what suffering I have endured." And she would turn around and lift her shirt to show me the criss-cross of scars on her back.

Xu Ma swore that the day that her young son could prepare an entire meal for himself and her mother-in-law—thereby fulfilling her duties to her husband's family—she would leave the village to go seek her fortune. This is how she came to be with the Chang family. Shortly after the birth of the second girl, Xu Ma left her home and hired herself out as a wet nurse for an orphanage that had been established in the Baoshan district by my Fourth Great-Uncle.

The year was 1936. My father's older sister had just been born, and her British governess, Mrs. Archer, needed a maidservant. So my grandmother spoke to her brother-in-law, and Fourth Brother sent a servant down to the orphanage for a clean and honest maid to live with a wealthy family in the city. Number 6 was recommended. But Number 6 happened to be out that week, and Xu Ma was substituting for her.

"I am Number 6," she announced, and, with no hesitation, followed Fourth Brother's servant to Shanghai.

For several years Xu Ma served as Mrs. Archer's maid, learning how to draw her bath with the correct temperature water and to cut her toenails with special British clippers. Then, in 1942, after Pearl Harbor, when my father's family was living in Hong Kong, the Japanese took over the city. Like other British citizens, Mrs. Archer was sent to a concentration camp. Xu Ma became the main nanny for the household and raised my father from birth.

"*Nong zang qi*," Xu Ma repeated to my father as a child and then again to us children. This meant that we had to go make something of ourselves. According to Xu Ma, we were being raised by her, a peasant woman who could barely read or write. If we did not grow up to be somebody, the whole Chang family would blame her.

27

How could I not love China when it came to me from Xu Ma's hands, hard and brown like the earth? I believed that Xu Ma's hands had tilled so many fields, cooked so many meals and scrubbed so many clothes that her palms and fingertips had taken on a distinct smell of their own, of dishwater, soil, scallions and ginger. They could do anything, those hands: split a chicken with one chop of a cleaver, make chrysanthemums bloom in the unyielding New England soil around our house, sew a pair of pants or a dress without consulting a pattern. Every day after school, Xu Ma would call me into her room to try on an article of clothing she was making me from scraps of material found in the remnant bin at the local fabric store. Across the top of my bed lay a blanket Xu Ma also made from bits of material, strips of unabashed color.

I wished I could be as accepted as Xu Ma by those around me, or perhaps accept myself as much as she accepted herself. She spoke only a few words of English but made jokes with the milkman every morning and traded gardening tips with my mother's friends. Everyone thought Xu Ma was my grandmother when we went out, and, holding on to her hand as we crossed the parking lot of the shopping mall, I felt safe from jeers of the teenagers. They never said anything when Xu Ma and I walked by, or if they did, I did not care because I felt Xu Ma's strength next to me. With her, I was grounded, safe from the treacherous crack that separated China and America. On my own, I skirted precariously the brink between the borders. When the other kids called me "Chink" or squashed their faces flat against their hands in imitation of my slanty eyes and broad nose, I stumbled inside and fell into the crack. From there, I stood outside China and looked on it with ridicule and ignorance.

Try as I might, on my own, I could not avoid the crevice between the cultures. I was surprised the first time the kids at school made fun of my favorite pair of pants, telling me that the legs were too short and the crotch hung too low. Xu Ma had made the pants for me, and I thought her clothes would protect me from unkind comments as they did for her. Afterward, I wore the pants only at home, and carefully scrutinized each article of clothing made by Xu Ma for possible defects. It hurt me to see China from my classmates' vantage point; it meant falling into the crack away from my Xu Ma.

So you see, I did not have bound feet. But, to my husband, they might as well have been bound because he thought I was old-fashioned and uneducated. I was only fifteen when I married him, which was early for a woman to leave her father's house, but something unlucky had happened to our family at the start of my seventh year: we became poor.

Now, as you know, we Changs are very proud people. We believe firmly in the Chinese saying, "Your reputation is your second life." This means that to lose your good reputation, your family name, is almost as bad as it is to lose life itself. We Changs lost everything when we were young, but we never lost the Chang name, and this was most important. We stayed together as a family and held on to our dignity, our *zhiqi*. Watch people when they win, and you will learn something. But watch them when they lose, and you will learn even more. Our misfortune made us strong, helped us become who we are today. Understand that and you will understand your bloodline.

Let me explain to you about sedan chairs. They look like chairs with two arms and a back, attached to long, bamboo carrying poles.

Sometimes the chairs have a little house with curtains built around them for privacy or to shield you from the sun. You settle yourself in the chair, and then the carriers, one in the front and one in the back, lift the poles to their shoulders and take you where you want to go. The bamboo poles are flexible, so the carriers balance both of them, one on each shoulder, and jog along at a quick pace that is bumpy in a soothing kind of way. When I was little we went around everywhere in sedan chairs. Very comfortable.

The carriers in Jiading all used to gather under a big tree right outside the walls of our compound and wait there for a fare. When Baba was summoned from the house on a medical emergency, for instance, a servant just ran out to the tree and hired a chair and three carriers. In emergencies, Baba needed three carriers because there was no time for the carriers to stop and change sides. The third carrier would run alongside the chair and take the weight upon his shoulder when one of the other two was tired.

I could tell a lot about a person from his sedan chair. First of all, by the color: the plain green bamboo for everyday use; the white cloth coverings and trimmings for funeral processions; and the red silks for the bride in wedding processions like the one I rode in the day I got married. Then, by the number of carriers—usually two— which signified the status of the occupant. Only officials were allowed to hire more than two bearers. This was the custom from the old days when society was divided into four classes: scholars, farmers, craftsmen and merchants. Scholars, who gave the world thought and order, were at the top. Farmers, who tilled the soil and gave the world food, followed. Then came craftsmen, who created the tools of livelihood. Merchants, who produced nothing but money for themselves, fell at the bottom of society. Even if merchants could afford to have several sedan chair carriers, they did not out of respect for the scholars.

In downtown Shanghai, where most of the city was governed

by the rules of the foreign settlements, no one paid attention to the old rules, and foreigners went around with as many bearers as they wanted, sometimes as many as four. I heard that there was one Chinese named Yang Zuqing who had four bearers and, strangely enough, all the bearers were foreigners! Yang Zuqing came from an old Shanghainese family and resented the presence of foreign settlements in Shanghai. To show the humiliation of Chinese people under foreign rule, he kept foreign bearers and paraded around the International Settlement with them. When he dismounted from the sedan chair, his foreign hirelings had to carry the fifteen-foot train of his specially tailored scholar's gown. It was said Yang Zuqing created a spectacle wherever he went. No wonder.

The two sedan chairs that my family owned were a sign of great honor upon our home. Most families only rented sedan chairs. Ours belonged to us: they were a present from the imperial court to Grandfather Chang when he was appointed to the office of provincial judge. Learned and impartial, Grandfather Chang had dispensed wisdom and logic in his rulings, and regularly rode to court in these chairs. After Grandfather Chang's death, my family kept the chairs under protective covering in a shed at the front of the house. We did not use the chairs except on special occasions, such as the wedding of First Cousin, which happened before I was born.

The eldest son of Baba's eldest brother, First Cousin was the most important family member in my generation. He stood in line to inherit the sedan chairs: Grandfather Chang had bequeathed the sedan chairs to his firstborn, First Uncle, and First Uncle, in turn, intended to give the sedan chairs to his firstborn, First Cousin. When First Cousin married, one of the sedan chairs was decorated with bridal red silks and dispatched to the neighboring province in order to fetch his bride. The second chair, which carried First Cousin in the procession, was decorated with the golden silks of Grandfather Chang's office in honor of our ancestor.

First Cousin's bride arrived in Jiading in the red sedan chair the day before the wedding. As part of her dowry, she brought with her magnificent jewels: jade, pearls and emeralds. I never saw the wedding but First Cousin's Wife told me all about it and would let me peek at her jewelry. She, First Cousin and their children lived in the rooms next to ours. Next door to them lived her own parents. Usually, a woman left her family behind when she married, but First Cousin's Wife had missed her own family so much when she first entered our household that First Cousin gave her permission to move her parents here. She and her parents spent most of the day together smoking opium, playing mah-jongg and talking mainly among themselves.

Now, you must know one other thing: that we were not all full-blood relations in my family house. Of the three brothers in my father's generation, only my Baba was Grandmother Chang's natural son. The two older brothers were sons of Grandfather Chang's first wife, who had died long ago. While Grandmother Chang had been only Grandfather Chang's second wife and lower in status than the first, Grandmother was now the oldest living family member. She, along with counsel from the oldest son, my First Uncle, headed the household.

But everyone knew that Grandmother Chang favored Baba and his family. Grandmother Chang continually said that Mama was the most talented of her daughters-in-law: Mama had borne eight sons from twelve children, the highest male birth ratio among the daughters-in-law. And whenever Grandmother Chang took meals in the privacy of her own bedroom, she always picked one of us children, usually Sixth Brother or me, to keep her company. The servant would pour out one cup of rice wine for her and a miniature cup for me. Years later in Shanghai, when I was throwing a dinner party for Second Brother, and Zhou Enlai came to eat, he was surprised at how much I could drink for a woman.

Our troubles began in 1907, right around New Year's, usually the most joyous period of the year.

I was dressed in my holiday clothes—a slippery red embroidered silk suit whose pants rustled as I walked—with my hair in tight braids that itched my scalp. As required for the New Year's festivities, I was on my best behavior, too. Back then, we believed that the gods watched over everything in the last months of the old year and the first months of the new year. Then they would decide what fortune and blessings to give out in the coming year. An accident as simple as a needle prick—mutilation of the body, which was a gift from the gods—could decide one's fate for the year. So, happily, my superstitious amah did not confine me to the women's quarters to sew, as was usually the case when I could not play in the courtyard. Instead, I was allowed to remain among my brothers and sisters. Sometimes, being careful not to spoil my red suit, I tried to help Mama in the kitchen.

The pantry had been stocked with rice, oil and other necessities so that we entered the new year prosperously, and the house was as neat as could be for the festivities. As we hung the New Year's banner in the front hall, Baba gave my brothers their annual lesson on the banner's four different characters: li, yi, lian, chi. They were to live their life by li, the Confucian rules of propriety. They were to conduct themselves with yi, righteousness. They were not to covet wealth or steal when serving in any public or private duty, lian. And they were to avoid any underhanded actions, chi. Most families welcomed the new year by displaying a banner with the four characters for fortune, rank, longevity and happiness. But we hung a banner with four different characters that were the guidelines for a scholar's family.

On the first day of the New Year's celebrations, the eighth day of the twelfth moon, the cooks from the three households joined together to prepare *congee* (rice porridge), special vegetables and a New Year's treat, barley soup with lotus seeds. We—uncles, cousins and all—were crowded around the holiday table eating our fill when my eldest brother, First Brother, accidentally knocked his rice bowl to the floor. The bowl broke into six pieces. Everyone, including the superstitious servants, insisted after a horrified pause, "No matter, no matter," to comfort First Brother. You see, it was actually a fairly serious matter that he had broken his rice bowl during the celebrations. In Shanghainese, the word for "rice bowl" sounds similar to the words for "sphere of influence," so when First Brother broke his rice bowl, he symbolically jeopardized his sphere of influence.

A "scholar-merchant," First Brother had completed his classical education but had not pursued the traditional route to a civil service post. He ran a cotton-oil factory and, for the most part, observed the practices of merchants. For instance, during the New Year's celebrations, he settled all his accounts before the year's end and always threw a feast with meat for all the workers on the sixteenth day of the twelfth moon. But lately First Brother had been having difficulties at his cotton-oil factory; that was why everyone was worried when he dropped his rice bowl. Several of First Brother's best workers had been lured away by a local comprador, a Chinese agent for a foreign trading concern, and the company was losing money while First Brother searched for replacements.

For that meal, First Brother took another rice bowl, but a servant carefully picked up the pieces of First Brother's rice bowl and set them aside for the neighborhood mender, who came by the house the next afternoon. With a small hand drill, the mender bored tiny holes into the broken pieces of the porcelain rice bowl and then sewed the bowl together with thin gold wire thread. Of course, the rice bowl looked very funny now, with a crisscross of gold wire on the white porcelain, but First Brother used this rice bowl from then on for the rest of the month. Only First Cousin teased First Brother about his clumsiness. First Cousin and First Brother did not always get along.

On the third night of the New Year's festival, I woke to the sound of people yelling and running around the house. Shaking awake First Sister, who could sleep through anything, I rushed out of bed. Outside, we found the entire family up, even First Cousin's Wife with her parents, and Grandmother Chang. Everyone was still in nightclothes. The women looked eerie in the moonlight with their hair loose and wild. Their feet were partially unwrapped, too, with the ends of the bindings dragging on the ground.

First Cousin's Wife's jewelry had been stolen! The servants lit up all the lanterns in our house. The neighbors from across the pond lit up all their lanterns. Then their servants came over and said they had seen a shadowy figure running across the roof of our compound. Both sets of servants searched well into the night, but the burglar and the jewels were nowhere to be found.

About a week or so after the robbery, First Brother's factory business suddenly took a turn for the better. His swift change of luck was surprising, and, in light of his rice bowl incident—when he supposedly damaged his sphere of influence—almost miraculous. So, of course, we rejoiced. Now perhaps this good fortune for our branch of the family was too much for First Cousin and his family to bear when they had just suffered a misfortune. Or perhaps there had always been trouble between First Cousin and First Brother. I do not know. But soon afterward I saw signs of their suspicion: First Cousin, his wife and her parents began to take dinner in their quarters. Their children were not allowed to play with us anymore.

One day First Brother walked by First Cousin's living quarters, and the mother of First Cousin's Wife spoke out bitterly: "Oh, there goes the thief."

When First Brother heard that comment, he hung his head and did not reply because he felt ashamed that his own good fortune had caused disharmony in the family. But Mama, who was sewing in our quarters next door, heard the accusation. That night she said to Baba that she would not remain in a house where people talked about her children in that manner.

Shortly before the end of the year Baba came into the room and announced to me and my brothers and sisters, "We are moving from here."

To save face, we left quietly and quickly at the start of the new year, packing our things and moving to a new town. It was very sad to leave Grandmother Chang, but she stayed behind in Jiading with the elder sons to maintain family unity. For several months we did not see her. Then Baba began to take some of us back to the Jiading house for an occasional meal. Baba visited the family home out of love and respect for his mother; he did not want her to lose face in front of the townspeople. As long as he periodically returned to Jiading, there at least appeared to be harmony in the Chang household.

The truth of the burglary surfaced only some ten years later. The thief turned out to be the son of Grandmother Chang's cook. His father, a faithful servant to Grandmother Chang, overheard his son bragging about the theft and confronted him. The son confessed to Grandmother Chang. He received a light prison sentence and provided the key to the mystery after so many years. During the search, he had hidden himself in one of the sedan chairs! None of the servants had thought to check the shed, much less look inside the sedan chairs.

In the ten years before our family name was officially cleared, we went through so much. We lost all our money. My brothers suffered as they pursued their education overseas. I had to get engaged at age thirteen. During those years my brothers, through their own achievements, slowly restored wealth and esteem to our family. But we were never the same: we could never return to the Jiading family home.

CHAPTER FOUR

BEAUTIFUL COUNTRY, BRIGHT NATION

At family gatherings growing up, I heard over and again tales of the Changs' achievements, their unity as a family, and their stature in China before the 1949 Communist Revolution. But only Yu-i ever told me the story of the sedan chairs. No one else ever spoke of it or passed the story on, as if it were a shameful secret. Had someone shared it with me, I believe I would have better understood the Changs. I would not have mistaken their pride for arrogance, or their desire to be above reproach as self-righteousness. As it was, I always wondered if I could measure up to their standards.

The episodes of Chang valor were like a living breathing memory to me, kept alive by stories passed from my father or Xu Ma, or all the relatives gathered around Fourth Sister's table. The Changs were wealthy but known for being above money. The Changs were smart and well connected but known for being above political intrigues. My father liked to tell of the long hours he spent out on the terrace riding his tricycle when Zhou Enlai, Communist Party liaison to the Kuomintang, and later the Prime Minister and Foreign Minister of the People's Republic of China, came to his family's house for discussions with members of the Kuomintang. In the mid-

1940s only the Chang home was considered neutral ground, a place where the two parties could meet informally and attempt to deal with the ideological differences between them.

My own grandfather, Eighth Brother, Chang Chia-chu, developed an innovative use for soybeans in the 1930s and founded the China Vegetable Corporation. His brother, Second Brother, Chang Chia-sen, formed the National Socialist Party, which still has a platform today in Taiwan. Fourth Brother, Chang Chia-ao, headed the Bank of China. I knew of the achievements of my "great" uncles long before I understood the term "great-uncle" as a measure of consanguinity.

Even after leaving China in 1949, the Changs excelled. My own grandparents, as far as I could tell, had not worked since coming to America from Brazil in the late 1960s, but continued to lead a lavish lifestyle in San Francisco. Fourth Brother taught at Stanford University, where a library reading room was posthumously dedicated to him at the Hoover Institution on War, Revolution and Peace. Second Brother continued to build support for his National Socialist Party. When Singapore became independent in 1965, Lee Kuan Yew, the first President of the country, invited Second Brother to Singapore to help him set up the government.

While proud of my grandfather and great-uncles, I did not know to what extent I dared identify with them. These were Chang men. Whenever the family talked about my great-aunts, the Chang women, they praised their successful marriages to educated or wealthy men, and their elegant skills in social situations. Chang women were clearly held to a different standard than the Chang men, and I worried where that left me, a first-generation Chinese-American girl who had never even been to China.

I thought that to be a Chang meant to be Chinese. I did not separate the two. I did not realize how many things were peculiar to the Chang family: their pride, their sense of righteousness. My mother's family was very well known in China, too—one of my Chinese teachers at Yale referred to them as the "Cutty Sark" family because they had developed a popular Chinese liquor, mao-tai, with which President Nixon was toasted when he first visited China in 1974—but members of her family rarely discussed their heritage to the extent the Changs did.

I hoped to achieve like my great-uncles. But the only time my grandparents ever referred to me as "a true Chang" was when they noticed how straight and tall I sat, "like a little princess," at a fancy Chinese restaurant. Or when they praised my high forehead in my "true Chang" face.

The message from the Changs was much clearer to my older brother. He was precocious and great things were expected of him. Once, when my parents were both graduate students and worked during the day, my grandfather, then visiting their home in Cambridge, asked my four-year-old brother, "Do you know Boston?"

My brother replied, yes, he did.

The next morning my grandfather took him on the subway to the center of Boston and looked at him expectantly. "Okay," he said. "Go ahead and show me Boston."

My brother looked perplexed.

"I thought you said you knew Boston," my grandfather said.

"I do." My brother straightened up proudly. "B-O-S-T-O-N."

At the time, my grandfather was actually disappointed in my brother. Later he repeated this story often to my brother as a joke, but always, it seemed to me, with the imbedded message that my brother did not fulfill the Chang expectations.

After the sedan chair incident, we moved to a small compound in the nearby town of Nanchang. While the old family compound in Jiading had boasted two courtyards and four doors that spanned the front, our new one had only one courtyard and two doors. Still, I liked it immediately because of an unusual feature in the pond at the back of the compound: a small wooden house shaped like a boat that rose on stilts amid the lily pads. Previously, the boat-house had been used as a spring tea pavilion, but there were so many of us that it became the children's quarters—one room for the boys, one for the girls, and another for the tutor who later joined us.

At the time of the move I was seven. Second and Fourth Brothers were studying in Japan, but our family, including the wives and children of First and Third Brothers, still numbered some seventeen people. This was a lot of mouths to feed. When we left Jiading it was the end of the year, usually a time of great celebration in the old family house: to usher in a prosperous new year, the servants would pile gold coins in jars and stock the kitchen with ducks, hams, rice and oil. But when we arrived in Nanchang we had nothing.

Then, the second or third evening in our new home, a man in the coarse cotton robes of a servant knocked frantically on our doors to ask if it were true that Baba was a doctor.

Baba said yes. The servant explained that he had come from one of the neighboring compounds, where his master had suddenly been taken ill. Could Baba forgive this disturbance during the holidays and come examine his master? Gathering his coat and medicine bag, Baba followed the servant out the door. Baba's healing powers must have been in good form, because when he returned home several hours later he called out to us and triumphantly produced four yuan from his pockets! The family rejoiced. We spent two yuan to buy our New Year's banner and kept the other two yuan in the house to usher in the new year.

So we began our new life in Nanchang. Luckily, we had not

moved so far away from the old family home that Baba had to find all new patients. He stayed in service to many of them but began to charge for his services. Too proud to demand his share of family holdings and the rent income from his brothers, Baba was now forced to support us from new earnings alone. Initially it embarrassed him to ask for money, but those patients who believed in our family's innocence—news of the robbery had spread quickly through the area—were happy to help Baba. Until now, Baba had never had to work solely in order to feed the family. This burden, as well as the emotional stress he suffered when leaving behind his mother and brothers, made him irritable and tired at times. In fact, I fear that in the end, the difficulties of this period of Baba's life contributed to his early death. Nevertheless, I shall never forget the dignity that Baba maintained in the years following our move.

That first year, it was Sixth Brother and I who went with Mama to pay our respects to her parents, as was Chinese custom at the beginning of each new year. The journey over bumpy country roads took about half a day from our new home. I remember what we wore. Sixth Brother and I were each in our own first set of fancy clothes. We felt so proud, he in his dark blue silk suit and me in my red. When we outgrew these suits, the younger brothers and sisters wore them. Until my family regained its fortune, these were the only fancy clothes among the children. Whichever child fit them best was allowed to go visiting with Mama and Baba.

Mama's parents were very good people. I called them Wai Po and Wai Gong, which, translated literally, means "Outside Grandmother" and "Outside Grandfather"; the mother's side is considered the "outside," as the Chinese trace lineage through the father's side. A Confucian scholar who tutored young boys in the area, Wai Gong spent several hours each day in his study in quiet contemplation, while Wai Po ran the household plainly, according to her husband's principles. She wore clothes of cotton, not silk, and rarely served meat at the table, only vegetables.

Mama's parents were the ones who had originally sold the house in Jiading to Grandfather Chang back when both sets of grandparents were good friends and Baba was promised to Mama. So when they heard the news of our move from this house and, in particular, the reason behind it, they were, of course, extremely sad. Wai Po's serene demeanor became vexed and troubled, and Wai Gong made a deep rumbling sound from his stomach, as if his insides had suffered a great disturbance.

Because it is considered thoughtless to cause one's parents concern, I was surprised when Mama told Wai Po and Wai Gong about the dissension in the family and our reduced circumstances. But her parents comforted her and counseled her. Wai Po and Wai Gong said that Mama's duties to the Changs lay in mending the rift. Calling upon the Five Confucian Virtues—*ren*, benevolence or humanheartedness; *yi*, righteousness or justice; *li*, propriety or decorum; *zhi*, wisdom, and *xin*, sincerity—they urged Mama to practice *ren* upon First Cousin, who had made the wrong accusation, and especially upon Grandmother Chang, who was surely missing Baba, her favorite son.

These words of wisdom Mama repeated to Baba when we returned from our three-day visit.

"According to Confucius, a man is a model to his family; the family, in turn, is an example to the state and to all citizens," Baba replied solemnly.

What Baba meant was that an accusation against First Brother was an indictment of Baba himself. When a son shamed his father, he disgraced the family in the eyes of the community and the nation. My poor Baba!

Here was a man who loved his country so much that he had

chosen the words "beautiful country, bright nation" for the Chang family. These words, *chia kuo pang ming*, were also intended by Baba to hold a second meaning. A play on almost identical sounds—*chia kuo pang min*—but with two different written characters, the family poem could also mean "from the family to the country to the people."

This second meaning of Baba's poem came from the book of the legendary Emperor Yao, who ruled for seventy glorious years after coming to the throne in 2357 B.C. A noble ruler, he was said to have been born with eyebrows of eight different colors. According to "The Book of Yao," the legendary Emperor Yao first cultivated himself. Then he became an example for his family, *chia*, who all became harmonious. From there, Emperor Yao and his family regulated the people of the domain, *kuo*, who all became brightly intelligent. Finally, he and they harmonized the myriad states of the empire, *pang*, and all the people, *min*, were transformed. The result was universal accord. Surely Baba had this idea in mind when he quoted Confucius about a man being a model for his family: he must have been very sad, feeling that he had somehow failed as a model to his family and, accordingly, to the state.

Mama urged Baba not to dwell on such thoughts. She said he had to consider Grandmother Chang's feelings, and perhaps, forgive First Cousin so there would be order in the larger Chang household. Baba pretended not to hear Mama and turned away, shaking his head. But that evening he retired to his study. For the next several days he stayed there in deep meditation. He even took his meals there. When finally he emerged, he called the family around him and told us that he had reached a decision of compromise. We would return to the Chang family house in Jiading for major holidays to pay respects to Grandmother Chang and to perform the rituals to the ancestors alongside the brothers. Otherwise, we would continue to live on our own in Nanchang.

No matter what our financial situation, Baba was determined that his sons' education would not suffer. With the first money he made after our move to Nanchang, Baba employed a tutor to live on the boat with the boys. Baba knew what was necessary for his sons' future: a solid grounding in Confucian studies and a modern education in Western subjects.

Since the fourth century in China, men had been recruited to fill important government posts through the state examination system. These extremely competitive exams took place on the provincial level every year, and the metropolitan level every several years. The subjects were usually poetry and rhymed prose, and there were always two or three thousand candidates. In the past in China, all anyone had to know were the Confucian classics to be able to gain a position and serve in the government. As a result, many young men who came from ordinary landlord and merchant families had been able to enter the government.

But certain reforms had been made in the government, and the centuries-old exam system, considered obsolete, had been abolished only a few years earlier. Since the second half of the last century, the best students had been sent abroad by the government (or even privately) to Japan, Europe or America to learn the ways of the West. Japan was considered like the West because it had defeated Russia in a war at the turn of the century. Now a new examination system, one which included subjects specifically for these students returned from the West, was being put into place.

Baba wanted very much for all of his sons to complete a classical education at home with tutors and then to attend the new-style schools that taught Western subjects, which would prepare them for further learning abroad. For instance, Second and Fourth Brothers studied German and French, respectively, at the Institute of Modern

Languages at Shanghai from age nine or ten. When we moved to Nanchang, Fourth Brother was studying finance and economics at Keio University; Second Brother, law and political science at Waseda University. Students at Japan's top universities, these two brothers were well on their way to prestigious positions in the Chinese government.

Schooling in both the classical and Western traditions was now necessary because they differed radically from each other. Confucius reached as far back as the eleventh century B.C., to the days of the Duke of Zhou, for his learning. His teachings stressed the restraint of man, such as the Three Bonds of Subordination that formed the basis of society, Man to Ruler, Woman to Man, and Son to Father. The lessons in Confucian training included the twenty-four examples of filial piety that we all adhered to. The Emperor of Shun, who had ruled from 2255 to 2208 B.C., was included in the *Xiao jing*, the Classic of Filial Piety, because he honored his parents even though they made several attempts to kill him.

The new schools that Fifth and, later, Sixth Brother attended were already following a different curriculum, one that included subjects such as geography and physics as well as teachings about equality among men, industrial progress and survival of the fittest. When Second Brother argued that my feet should not be bound, he had called upon his Western training.

At that time China's new-style schools were dominated by a single personality, Liang Qichao. He introduced to China the concept of constitutional monarchy as well as other radical ideas. I remember how my Fifth and Sixth Brothers used to line up to buy his newspapers and readings. Second Brother joined Liang Qichao's political party while he was in Japan. Later, Liang Qichao became my husband's mentor.

Each morning after Mama and the cook had walked back across the gangplank of our little houseboat with the trays of empty breakfast dishes, classes began for my brothers. They sat in a row, four or five of them at one long table. Sometimes, if we were not needed in the kitchen, we girls sat at another table on the side, waiting for the tutor to come by if he was not busy with the boys.

The few books I learned were the Confucian classics for little children like the *Xiao jing,* which I mentioned before, and the *Xiao xue,* the Book of Moral Training. Of course, my education was nowhere as severe as that of my brothers. I just sat in class and copied from the primer a few times for the tutor, while my brothers had not only to copy but to memorize hundreds of lines from the *Analects of Confucius* and the *Book of the Golden Mean.* The room was filled with the sounds of their chanting as they attempted to memorize their lessons. The chanting became more intense as they raced through their lesson, hoping to learn each passage by heart, anxiously anticipating their turn. At any moment the tutor could call on one of them and demand a recital, or *bei shu,* which, translated literally, meant "back to the book."

My brothers were also subject to Baba's strict eye. Each morning as he dressed, Baba would have one of the brothers kneel in front of a burning incense stick. There, my brother would have to *bei shu* until the incense stick burned down in front of him. Eighth Brother, your grandfather, told me that sometimes, when he did not know his lessons well, he would sway back and forth on his knees and blow air onto the incense stick as he chanted so that it would burn faster.

You children in the West play until you are five or six. But my brothers began with tutors at age four or so, and from this early age they were expected to comport themselves as scholars. They could not play with toys, arrows or soldiers, and were not supposed to mix with certain people. For instance, whenever Mama and her friends gathered to play mah-jongg, Mama sent all the brothers, even the youngest, out of the room. She did not want them to get interested in gambling. Also, scholars supposedly brought them bad luck, they said, because the word for scholar, *dushuren*, was a homonym for "losing at gambling."

Though my brothers all had very good dispositions, they were still boys and liked to play. One time in the house in Jiading, my mother walked by the outhouse and heard noises. Peering into the window, she saw that Second Brother and Fourth Brother had laid a board across the holes and were gambling at dice while their tutor sat waiting for them to return from the toilet.

"What are you doing in there?" Mama scolded through the window. "What a disgrace! Return to your studies at once!"

Second and Fourth Brothers hurried from the outhouse and stood before Mama with their heads hung in shame as they received their scolding. When Baba returned that evening, he was also very angry. He threatened to punish them with memorization of fifty chanted verses each by the following morning. Only Grandmother Chang stepped in to save the brothers that evening.

She reminded my parents that sometimes even the best boys strayed, like the great philosopher Mencius during his boyhood. Mencius's mother is said to have moved their house from the neighborhood of a cemetery when she noticed her son playing there. Later, it is said, the family moved from a house near the market when she noticed him wasting time at shops. Finally, they moved to a home near a school, so everything was fine.

I am not a learned woman. Look at my Chinese writing; you can see that it is not a scholarly hand. And there are many characters I do not know. Being learned in Chinese is not like being learned in English. If I were learned, I would be able to write in classical

Chinese, which is nothing like spoken Chinese. It is completely different.

But I did learn simple things like how we had to obey the Three Bonds of Subordination: man to ruler, son to father and woman to man. We had to respect the Five Reverent Tiers: Heaven, Earth, Emperor, Family and Teacher. This is how I knew that when my husband fell in love with the woman his mentor's son was supposed to marry he sinned against the Teacher.

CHAPTER FIVE

A GIRL'S EDUCATION

As a child, I heard a great deal about the schooldays of my father and my great-uncles, and they all became entwined in a way that made me think that suffering as a student was good. My father said that when Second and Fourth Brothers were studying in Japan and the family stopped sending them so much money, the two brothers were so poor they had to buy one book at a time, study it, then return it to buy another. Likewise, they could only afford one washcloth and had to cut it in half.

When I was in school I was the only one in my class who covered my textbooks with brown paper bags although I could have bought any book covers I liked. Similarly, I used my first washcloth until it had a hole in the middle. Then I pasted it into my scrapbook for remembrance. So powerful were these stories of my family's self-sacrifice.

My father told me that Yu-i once visited our house in Connecticut in the early 1970s when she had just moved to America. Afterward she wrote to my grandfather in San Francisco, her brother, complimenting my parents on the fact that each of us children had a desk and proper light by which to study. My father was very proud and relieved when my grandmother read Yu-i's letter to him.

Whenever we visited my grandparents in San Francisco, we were given a little assignment. Sometimes we visited the graves of Second and Fourth Great-Uncles. Once we were sent out onto a bridge in the middle of Chinatown to copy down the Five Confucian Virtues, written on bronze plaques along the walls of the bridge. I wrote the stories down in English in the same notebook I used for my drawings of horses. As we were copying the Virtues, an old Chinese man who seemed my grandfather's age came up and praised us, "Very good. Very good. This you must know."

My mother was an educator too, and we always did our homework in the kitchen as she prepared food. She would make a lesson out of everything; baking, for instance, meant the adding of fractions.

In junior high and high school, I was supposed to return from school and work on my homework immediately so that, when my mother came home, I could ask her any questions I had in, say, calculus or geometry, before dinner. Whatever my mother could not answer, she referred to my father. Then, after dinner, I was expected to study some more.

One night my mother came up to check on my studies. I had a big exam the following day in calculus, and my parents had been helping me all week to prepare. When my mother came up the stairs, she found me planning my outfit instead of studying for the following day.

My mother was furious. "What is wrong with you?" She was so disappointed in me that she could barely speak to me for the entire weekend after the test.

51

When his family left China in 1949, my father lived in Japan and, later, in Brazil. Six years after he left China, he attended a prep school on Long Island where, as one of the few Chinese at the school, he was expected to perform. Indeed, he and the only African-American at the school graduated at the top of their class.

After high school my father went to M.I.T. One of his jobs was at the cafeteria where he had to collect the trays and plates after meals and stack them for cleaning. Some boys from Hong Kong used to dump food on their trays, smear it, and deliberately make a mess for him. They knew who his family had been in China and said that he was only playing at being poor. I asked my father how he felt being treated that way. He said he thought of this all as water rolling off a duck's back. He did not let it affect him.

I wished I had that kind of resilience. Both my mother and father sincerely believed that Chinese were as good as, if not better than, non-Chinese. Whenever my father's colleagues at Yale bragged about having descendants off the *Mayflower*, my father would just smile mildly, as if amused at the comparative youth of America's history. Both my parents referred to non-Chinese as *waiguoren*, meaning "foreigners."

Before she came to America, my mother told me, she used to look at pictures of *waiguoren* in magazines and think, How ugly. Surrounded by them on the SS *President Wilson* when she came from China to America in 1949, she regarded them as big, hairy and white as ghosts. The first night as she and her family sat at dinner, foreigners at a table next to them were eating peach Melba. My mother, who was then nine, said she and her sisters had heard that everything was bigger in the West.

"Look," they said to one another, pointing at the neighboring table, "look at the giant fried eggs that the barbarians are eating!"

Even after hearing these stories, I still longed to be accepted by my white peers. I remember one day coming home from school crying because the kids there, one boy in particular, named Douglas, were teasing me.

"Ching-chang-chong," Douglas would call out the minute the teacher left the room.

"Ching chong, wing wong," he chanted in the hallway, cafeteria and schoolyard. From his desk all day long, whenever the teacher was not looking, Douglas made faces at me, his eyes and nose squashed flat against his hands.

My father offered to teach me a comeback that would shut Douglas up for good, make him crawl away in silence. It was the worst thing in the world I could call anyone, so bad that I had to promise never to use the word again. "You just call Douglas, 'You white turtle egg,'" my father said menacingly. It took me a few minutes—far longer than the instant I knew this insult would not work on Douglas—to understand that "turtle egg" was the translated Chinese version of "son of a bitch." My father explained to me that many different males fertilized a female turtle's eggs before she hatched them. To my father, a turtle egg was bad enough, but a *white* turtle egg was the worst.

I never told my father that I did not follow his advice about Douglas, just as I never told my mother how wrong she had been in response to my complaints. The one time I told her that the kids at school sang out, "Ching chong, ching chong" when I walked by, she said to me, laughing, "They're probably just trying to speak Chinese to you. You should feel sorry for them. Listen. They can't even get the words right." And when I explained to her that they were making fun of me, she frowned, perplexed, and asked, "I think any time they say stupid things you should just turn to them and say, 'I bet you just wish you were Chinese. Like me.'"

At the time, my parents seemed incredibly naive with their advice. I realize now it was their pride trying to guide and protect me.

Second and Fourth Brothers returned from Japan in 1909. Fourth Brother took a position on the board of Posts and Communications and contributed his salary to the family. He also took over the household budget and approached Mama about a relevant issue: too many unsettled children in the family. Of the twelve children, five of the brothers and all four of the sisters were still unmarried. Mama should begin working in earnest on the future of the girls, Fourth Brother suggested.

The fortuneteller was called to the house to consult the horoscope of my fourteen-year-old sister, First Sister. Because she was the eldest daughter, it was important to settle her marriage plans before everyone else's. The fortuneteller read First Sister's *bazi*, the eight characters based on First Sister's name and the time, day, month and year of her birth. When Mama and First Sister emerged from their session with the fortuneteller, they looked worried. First Sister was in tears and quickly retreated to the girls' quarters.

Mama announced matter-of-factly, "First Sister is not to be married for many years. The fortuneteller said she must marry only after she turns twenty-five, or else her husband will die prematurely."

I was Second Sister, and I replaced First Sister in line for marriage. That was how I came to be the one who married Hsü Chih-mo.

Years later, in 1921, when I was already married to Hsü Chih-mo and had left China to join him in England, First Sister became very close to my mother-in-law. Still waiting to marry, First Sister would pass the time in the countryside with my mother-in-law—bring her presents, play mah-jongg and amuse her with stories about different people from Shanghai. Hsü Chih-mo and I divorced in 1922 when First Sister was twenty-six and free to marry. It was a few months later that my mother-in-law said with regret to Mama, "Maybe we should have married this one instead."

My mother-in-law did not mean to be unkind. Fate is just strange that way; perhaps First Sister should have been the one who married Hsü Chih-mo instead. But in that case I know there also would have been a divorce between the two of them. First of all, the Hsü family would not have appreciated how freely First Sister spent money. Secondly, First Sister did not care at all about books or schooling. Hsü Chih-mo wanted an educated woman.

I was about ten when the fortuneteller read First Sister's *bazi*, and, learning of my own fate to marry young, I felt my carefree days were numbered. As soon as I married, I would have to serve my husband's family and bear children.

I wanted to learn but Mama said Baba would not pay for a girl to study. My father was forward-looking for his sons but did not have enough money to worry about the cost of his daughters' education. I think that if we had not become poor and my father had not had to worry so much about the cost of education for his eight boys, then maybe he would have been more generous about getting me my own tutor, or letting me study at the best schools like the women my husband later loved.

Where my desire to study came from I do not know. In Mama's day, a woman never left the inner chambers of her quarters until she took leave of her father's house to marry. Moving in with her husband and in-laws, she traded one confinement for another. It was unthinkable for a girl to pursue learning outside the home. "If a girl is ignorant that is her virtue," the saying went; an uneducated girl was more obedient to her husband's family.

At that time we lived next door to a family whose two daughters attended a modern girls' school in Shanghai. Each morning, before catching the train, the girls donned their school uniforms: brown pants and brown shirts with no collars. During her annual visit to our house, the matchmaker said the girls were pretty and learned. Surely one of them was suitable for the Chang boys. But Mama, whose robes all had high collars that covered the neck, wrinkled her face in distaste. "Such display of the neck is inexcusable," she declared. "Those modern girls will never marry one of our sons."

Of the four girls in the family, I was the one who cared the most about education, even from the very beginning. First Sister only cared about pleasing people and playing mah-jongg; later on, she became addicted to opium. Third Sister loved food and cooking; that is why she was the fattest. And Fourth Sister, who was born a few years after we moved to the Nanchang house and is now a clothes designer, cared mainly about art and design. After our family's fortunes improved, she had a tailor come to the house every day and make her new clothing.

I think my desire for education was due to the fact that I knew that I had been born into changing times. Also, I admired my Second and Fourth Brothers very much. And I was the first in my family among the girls not to have bound feet. First Sister, who was only two years older than I, had bound feet but absolutely no patience for books and learning.

The two women that my husband fell in love with after me were only about two years younger than I, but they were much better educated. Like me, they did not have bound feet. I think that, beginning with my generation, more and more women wanted to get educated because the ways of the West were becoming known in China.

In 1912, when I was twelve, my little sister, the twelfth and final child, was born, and I was needed at home to care for her. I was quiet as I helped Mama, chewing the rice for Fourth Sister and minding her play, but I still thought about my schooling.

One day, when Fourth Sister was about six months old, I found an advertisement in the Shanghai *Shengbao* about a girls' school in Suzhou called the Teachers' College Preparatory School. For the first three years, a girl took classes. Then, in the fourth year, she practiced teaching younger students, ending up with a primary teacher's certificate. The school taught the new Western subjects and, best of all, charged only five yuan a term. This included room, board, book money, spending money, and even train fare to and from Suzhou for the holidays. Incredibly cheap. I was certain Baba would be willing to pay for that.

I brought up the idea with Mama. After she heard the price, the first thing she asked me was whether the school uniforms had collars or not. I told her that the advertisement had said nothing about uniforms. Then Mama said that Suzhou was too far away, that she would not let me live away from home alone. A city located about one hundred miles west of Shanghai, Suzhou was known for its gardens of unusual rock formations and for its beautiful women. According to a saying, Suzhou women, with their lustrous skin and lilting accents, could ask a man for anything.

Determined to find someone to accompany me to Suzhou, I somehow convinced First Sister to attend school. To this day I do not know how I did it; she loved to be idle and had no interest in studies. Still, she was very agreeable and, as she was not going to be married for many years, she had nothing else to do with her time. Gaining Mama's permission to approach Baba, I went to him and asked if he would pay for First Sister and me to go to this school.

Baba had always said educating girls was too expensive, but he could not complain about this particular school: it was so inexpensive. It was almost cheaper for him to send us to school than to keep us fed at home, I think. After some thought, Baba agreed to send us to Suzhou. Just as the matter seemed settled, I learned that the school required an entrance examination.

"What are we going to do?" First Sister asked me. We had only studied a little with a tutor at home and did not think that we knew anything. But we had to get into this school; it was the only one we could afford.

Two of our cousins, Second Uncle's daughters, were already attending school. They were smart, First Sister said. Maybe they could take the exam for the two of us.

Maybe we could prepare for the exam together, I suggested to First Sister, but she shook her head. She was only going to school to keep me company, and she did not want to have to study. She said that if one of the cousins did not take the exam for her she would surely fail.

So the next time Baba visited Jiading, he asked the two older cousins to take the exam for First Sister and me under our names. I still do not know why he compromised his usual high moral standards to make this request but, thankfully, he did, and my cousins agreed. I told First Sister that she and I should at least try to pass the test on our own. So she and I also took it, but under our cousins' names. This way, if First Sister and I failed, it did not matter.

As it was, all four of us passed the exam. First Sister laughed and said she had guessed at most of the answers, but I was so relieved.

Our cousins gave their names and passing scores to two girls we all met after the exam. These girls had not passed and were extremely grateful for such help from strangers. I never did find out how those girls managed in school under my cousins' names.

Crying the morning we left, Mama sent one servant on the train to Suzhou with First Sister and me. When we reached the campus of the school, First Sister groaned.

"It's so big," she said. Her feet were bound. "How am I going to walk around here?"

First Sister and I were put in the same room on the second floor of the dormitory building. We shared it with four other girls, three of whom also had bound feet like First Sister. The four of them were always complaining about the size of the campus, which I thought was actually very small. There were only three buildings: the dormitory, the classroom, and the dining hall. Meals were extremely simple, four or five dishes with a big bowl of white rice set in the middle of a round table. Ten of us sat together at a table for these meals. First Sister said Baba would never have hired these cooks at home, and she was always writing Mama to send food, but I ate what I could because I did not want Baba's five yuan per term to go to waste. Even at that low price, we did have school uniforms, blue apronlike smocks that we put on over our regular clothes. Mama was pleased when she learned that our necks were covered.

There were about forty girls at the school, many of them with bound feet. Almost all of them were at least three years older than I. I was only twelve. We studied geography, math, history and literature. The teachers were men who carried rulers as they strode about the classroom during lessons. They did not hit us, but they rapped the desk with the ruler whenever a student recited her lessons incorrectly. Unlike First Sister, I worked hard. Only one other student at school studied as hard as I. This girl had normal feet too. She once said to me that our school was so cheap, the teachers had to be lenient; otherwise, the students would leave.

Classes began at eight-thirty in the morning. We rose at seven, made our beds, put on our uniforms, ate a quick breakfast and walked across the small yard to the classes to prepare our lessons before the teacher arrived. I would always carry First Sister's books and try to match my own step to her mincing ones. It saddened me to see First Sister in such pain, but in many ways, she had it easier than I at school because the teachers were more lenient with her. I do not know why, but it seemed the teachers at my school were less strict with the girls with bound feet. Maybe the teachers thought these girls were old-fashioned and unable to learn.

First Sister was smart but never studied. She always seemed to be doing something for her friends—even washing or mending their clothes—instead of looking at her books. Whenever she answered incorrectly in class, the teachers said, "Oh, that's okay." But if I was wrong the teachers would rap the ruler and say, "Now how could that be?"

We were so different, First Sister and I. She never worried about the future. I always thought about tomorrow and considered my studies or my work as important as my games. When First Sister finally did marry, shortly after my divorce, she chose a wealthy man with an unstable family background and absolutely no education. I was living in Germany at the time and wrote her that it was a bad idea, that if the money ran out there would be nothing to fall back on. She said that he had so much money—his family owned commercial lots and a theater in Shanghai—that it would never run out. For about fifteen years they lived very well. First Sister bore a healthy son. Her husband did not gamble. He kept his title deeds piled on top of a huge wardrobe that stood against one wall of their room. Each month, he threw the sacks of cash from their rents into the wardrobe.

Then one day in 1937 or 1938, First Sister came to see me. I was working as vice-president of the Shanghai Women's Savings Bank then and had a desk at the far back of the bank where I could oversee everything. First Sister hobbled the entire length of the room on her bound feet and sat in front of me in tears. She said that she had been too scared to tell me earlier, but for the past year her husband had been gambling like a madman, playing a game with thirty-two dominoes called *tuipaijiu*. At first he won. But now he had started to lose. And whenever he lost, he would reach into the wardrobe, pull out a bag of money and throw it on the table to begin another round. Neither she nor her son could stop him. He had gone through all the money and was now starting to reach for the title deeds on top of the wardrobe. A fortuneteller had told her that when the last title deed was gone her husband would die.

First Sister wanted me to get the deeds from him and put them in the bank's safe. Normally I would not have gotten involved, but from our schooldays together I was used to taking care of First Sister in some way. I also worried about her husband; all along I had thought him wrong for her.

I went to First Sister's husband and told him that I wanted the remaining title deeds from the top of the wardrobe. He would not give them to me. He said he needed them in order to pay for the education of his concubine's daughter. I did not believe him, but nodded and pretended as if I did. A week later I returned. I lied and told him that I had paid for the daughter's education.

"Give me at least one title deed," I then insisted. "That will be the last title deed, the one you must not use. I will put it in my bank."

He did not check the truth of my story; he gave me the single title deed. But a few months later he appeared at the bank. He looked haggard and weak. "Give it to me," he said, and I knew he would not leave the bank without his deed. I ended up giving it to him; who could argue with a man like that, so desperate that he threatened to kill himself? Shortly thereafter he died in his sleep, just as the fortuneteller who had read First Sister's fortune predicted. So, who knows, perhaps my sister's fate was worse than mine.

CHAPTER SIX

PLUM BLOSSOM
IN SNOW

When I was eleven years old, long before I had dated or kissed a boy, I dreamed that a young white man with wavy brown hair walked into the room.

He strode toward me where I sat on the couch and enveloped me in his arms, embracing me with a soft, fleshy kiss. I gave in to him. I kissed him back with passion and fervor. Then something shifted in me. I summoned all my self-control and pushed him firmly toward the door.

"No, I must marry a Chinese," I said.

When I woke up, I was flushed and aroused. Over and over, I recalled the kiss with the white man, that one moment when I had given in to my desires. What freedom I felt! What joy to kiss the white man! My eleven-year-old imaginings had never known such liberty or bliss. I did not dwell on the other aspect of my dream, pushing the man away. But already there was conflict.

I always thought of my parents as very modern. Their friends were non-Chinese. They spoke perfect unaccented English. But the message when I was growing up was that I should try to marry a Chinese person.

Whenever I admired some painting in the house or lovingly dusted some piece of oriental furniture in the living room, my father would say, "Someday when your mother and I pass along, you'll get this piece . . . if you marry a Chinese." Half-breed versus pure breed, my father further explained, talking about people as if they were dogs. I had to marry a Chinese to carry on the Chang bloodline, to give birth to pure Chinese children.

Whenever my father spoke about pedigree and racial purity, my mother would giggle uncomfortably and say reassuringly, "Don't listen to your father. You just marry who you love."

My mother never said, though, that we children should *not* marry Chinese people. I believe she expected the best of both worlds to occur: that we would marry whom we loved and they would just happen to be Chinese. We meaning my brother and myself. Early on, from the time of her crushes on the star of "The Six Million Dollar Man," Lee Majors, and other American actors, my sister excluded herself from having to marry a Chinese.

"She's just hopeless," my father would comment on the chances of her marrying a Chinese. That left just me of the girls to carry on the Chang bloodline, to give birth to pure Chinese children and not mix our blood with any non-Chinese.

My parents always said that having "similar values" was the key to their marriage. Growing up, I never really understood what they meant. As far as I could tell, my parents were quite different from each other. Both were intelligent, but my father's approach to a problem was slow and deliberate, while my mother's was quick and intuitive. When my father got mad, he blew up in a huge storm and then forgot about it ten minutes later; my mother stewed in anger for days, even weeks. My father came from Hong Kong and Shanghai, two cosmopolitan cities; my mother came from a mountainous province in western China called Guizhou, which was known for being poor and backward. Guizhou has no indigenous salt, and the Shanghainese like to joke, "The people from Guizhou have to hang a piece of salt over the table and look up at it as they eat."

But for all their differences, their values were deeply shared and conveyed to us children in our upbringing. For instance, in order to teach us discipline, the value of time, and the incremental nature of improvement, my parents made us practice our musical instruments—me and my brother the piano, and my sister the violin—every day. For each hour we practiced per week, we were allowed one half hour of television. Whenever guests came to the house, we were required to perform for them.

My father had a theory about life, that everything went along as was but for certain crucial moments in time, and if you did not perform correctly or choose wisely at those moments, you lost that turning point forever. This theory applied to planning a career, finding a spiritual path and, of course, choosing a mate. So, even though I daydreamed about Clint Eastwood and Sean Connery (and secretly liked the hair on their bodies), I always thought that when the crucial moment came I would do the right thing. I would push the non-Chinese man away and say, "No, I must marry a Chinese."

I did in fact want to marry a Chinese—to be a good girl, to honor my parents' wishes—yet did not limit myself to Chinese men as I began to date. When I was twenty-one I fell deeply in love with a non-Chinese but astonished myself when I broke off the relationship and pronounced the very words from my dream: "I would marry a Chinese just to please my father."

No one, including my father, had ever demanded this of me, but so strongly did I feel the expectation that I actually believed my sacrifice would make me a stronger, better, more contented person. Instead, I felt torn in two, more uncertain than ever of whom I might find to love.

I was thirteen years old when I heard my husband's name for the first time. Mama and Baba called me into the living room when I was home from school during the holidays and handed me a small silver picture case.

"What's this for?" I wanted to know.

Look at his picture, they said. I opened the case and saw a photograph of a young man with a big head, a protruding chin and round, wire-rimmed glasses.

Baba wanted to know what I thought of the man in the picture.

I closed the case quietly. Since the reading of First Sister's fortune, I had been expecting this moment. I turned to Baba and replied carefully, "It has nothing to do with me."

This was how it was at that time according to Chinese tradition: I would marry the man my family chose for me.

His name was Hsü Chih-mo. Fourth Brother had found him for me. As secretary to the provincial governor of Zhejiang, part of Fourth Brother's official duties was to inspect area schools. At the Hangzhou Middle School a few weeks earlier, he had been extremely impressed by one student's composition. Entitled "On the Relationship Between Fiction and Society," the essay was an impeccable imitation of Liang Qichao, one of the leading intellectuals of the time and a good friend and colleague of Second Brother's. As Fourth Brother later explained, he had leafed through hundreds of schoolboys' efforts to imitate Liang Qichao, but none before had caught his style, his elegant blend of classical and colloquial Chinese.

The calligraphy of the young writer also revealed extraordinary talent. Examining the form of each individual character, Fourth Brother noted that the *gu*—the strength of the stroke, the emphasis of the brush against the paper at every line, hook and curve—exhibited steadfast purpose and direction. The *qi*—the natural spirit of the characters that a man achieved only by training for years and then discarding all his learning at the correct moment—spoke of vision and integrity.

Inquiring about the young scholar whose essay so impressed him, Fourth Brother learned that he was the only son of a very good and wealthy family in the area. Fourth Brother did not need to know more. That evening he sent a letter of introduction to the head of the Hsü household. Using his formal name, Chang Chia-ao, Fourth Brother suggested a match between Hsü Chih-mo and me. Shortly thereafter, Hsü Chih-mo's father sent a note personally approving the match. Fourth Brother had already begun to earn a reputation in the area and to restore our family name to one of wealth and esteem. Hsü Chih-mo's father wrote very simply: "I, Hsü Shen-ju, would be honored to have Chang Chia-ao's sister." And that is how Hsü Chih-mo and I became engaged.

Years later, when I was already married and living with Hsü Chih-mo's family, one of the servants told me what had happened when Hsü Chih-mo saw my picture for the first time.

He turned down the corners of his mouth and said with distaste, "Country bumpkin."

So he did not care for me from the very beginning. But even he, who became modern later, did not dare to defy tradition. He obeyed his father and married me.

At that time in China, we married whoever our parents chose for us. This was another sign of our filial piety, perhaps one of the most extreme: in a complete sign of obedience, proper young men and women became betrothed to each other at their parents' wishes and met each other only on their wedding days. The *Liji*, *The Book of Rites*, said: "Marriage is to make a union between two persons of different families, the object of which is to serve, on the one hand, the ancestors in the temple, and to perpetuate, on the other hand, the coming generation."

But marriages like this did not mean that there was no love. The love just came afterward. First, duty to the parents, the family and the spouse, then love would follow.

You might think that the tradition of "free choice" that you have in the West—when two individuals pick each other—is a smarter way to meet people. I would disagree. Young people can get carried away. Nowadays, I think you people take too long to learn everything about the person first until it becomes impossible to separate the good points from the bad. Then you decide not to marry. This is the problem with "free choice." No one is perfect.

In the Chinese way, your parents have your best interest in mind. For instance, my parents had entrusted Fourth Brother with the reponsibility of choosing a husband for me, and I trusted Fourth Brother's decision. I think normally this responsibility would have fallen to First Brother, but after the burglary incident he became so depressed that he turned to opium and could not be relied upon as a leader of his generation. So the task fell to Fourth Brother and the way he chose a husband for me was very normal. We did not have to know Hsü Chih-mo's height or whether his house had twenty servants or a hundred. We only needed to know about his family reputation, his education, and his temper. These are the three things you must examine about a mate. That is all you need to know.

For instance, none of us Changs knew your mother when your father decided to marry her in 1961. Eighth Brother, your grandfather, was living in Brazil at the time and had never met the woman his son would marry. He knew only that his son's fiancée was studying biology in college and came from the Hua family of Guizhou, known for the development of mao-tai. This is the liquor that Grandmother Chang used to drink when we were little. Eighth Brother also knew that the father of his son's fiancée worked for the United Nations in New York City. So the two things your grandfather knew were family reputation and education. He had to call me to inquire about her temper. I was the first Chang family member to meet your mother and her family. They were visiting Hong Kong one summer on home leave, and I was still living there. I received them in my house near the Peak and watched very carefully how your mother acted, how she sat, how she poured tea and interacted not just with me but with her own parents. She was very sweet and even-tempered, and when I reported this to Eighth Brother he was satisfied.

I am called the spy of the family because I know many people and always try to find out as much about the family involved as possible. My granddaughter met her husband through me—I played mah-jongg with his mother, who was very fair—so I knew it was a good match. And your mother and father have a very strong marriage. If you or your brother or sister want to meet anyone or know about anyone, you ask me. A good match is very hard to find on your own.

Before my engagement to Hsü Chih-mo could be considered official, a fortuneteller had to come to the house to compare our *bazi*—the eight characters based on each of our names, and the times, days, months and years of our births—for compatibility. Sitting between Mama and the fortuneteller, I waited anxiously to learn about my future with Hsü Chih-mo.

The fortuneteller looked at her charts.

"I like this family," she said. "Very good family."

Peering again at her charts she began to explain to Mama about the birth years involved. Hsü Chih-mo was four years older than I. His year of birth, 1896, corresponded to the sign of the Monkey in the twelve-year cycle. When an emperor of the Tang Dynasty sent an envoy to India to obtain the sacred books of the Buddhist religion, he chose the Monkey as man's companion for the important mission. Charming and amusing, the Monkey was the first animal deified by the Buddhists. But, the fortuneteller said, the Monkey could also get tricky and ugly.

The Rat, my birth sign, symbolized industry and prosperity. The Rat was a scavenger who could locate, acquire and hoard abundant supplies of food. At the same time, however, the Rat could act timid and mean.

Taking a deep breath, the fortuneteller addressed Mama directly. "I must tell you that I feel the Rat and the Monkey are not suitable mates in this instance," she declared. "It would be better if your daughter was a Dog, a symbol of fidelity."

"My two eldest girls," Mama responded with dismay. "The first cannot marry until she is twenty-five and now this second one is not suited for the man."

I could barely contain myself. What was wrong? I wanted to know but did not dare interrupt Mama and the fortuneteller. Was it something wrong with me? Or was it something wrong with Hsü Chih-mo? What did the fortuneteller mean when she said we were not suitable?

Mama shook her head and looked at me almost impatiently. "What are we going to do? One of you must marry soon."

For a long moment, Mama was silent, then she shrugged her shoulders as if in resignation. "We must do what we have to," she said.

So the fortuneteller changed me from a Rat to a Dog—making my year of birth 1898 instead of 1900—and declared the match propitious. My family delivered this message to the Hsüs without mentioning the switch of my birth year. A week later a pair of ducks, symbols of marital fidelity, appeared at the door from the Hsüs. Our family accepted them. The engagement was official.

What misfortune surrounded my marriage is one of the great mysteries of my life. I always wondered exactly what unluckiness the fortuneteller had seen in her charts before making me a Dog. Had she foreseen our divorce? I never understood why Mama obeyed the fortuneteller when it came to First Sister, but not to me. Did Mama think it was all right for me to marry an unsuitable mate? Was it just fate that Hsü Chih-mo and I would marry despite the unlucky forecast?

I am not so sure you can escape your fate. Look at what happened with my First Sister. Who knows? Maybe a ghost spirit lingered in her charts.

After another consultation with the fortuneteller that only Mama attended, the wedding date was set for a year and a half later, November 1915. In accordance with the tradition for proper Chinese men and women, Hsü Chih-mo and I would meet for the first time on that day.

The Hsüs did not want the wedding to take place until after Hsü Chih-mo's graduation from middle school. I still had another year and a half before finishing my classes and then one more year until I would receive my primary school teacher's certificate, but neither the Hsüs nor my parents considered my schooling. The Hsüs did not mention it, while my parents told me to withdraw from school immediately to prepare for my wedding.

"A girl's schooling does not matter," they said. "The purpose of a girl's life is to marry. You must remain at home and prepare yourself for your destiny."

I liked school. Also, I knew that Hsü Chih-mo was very educated, and I wanted to learn up until my wedding date. It took me a long time to convince my parents to let me return to school for another year. The main reason they let me go was to keep First Sister busy until her twenty-fifth birthday—still several years away—and First Sister would not attend school unless I did.

Unfortunately, after I got engaged and returned to school for a full year before my wedding, the teachers became lazy with me, not bothering to correct me if I answered wrong. Even the strict mathematics teacher, who had once regarded me as one of his favorites, now spoke to me as if nothing that he taught me mattered. He knew I would be leaving them in no time. Girls were always dropping out of my school when they got engaged; I was one of the very few who returned after my engagement. I think girls were only sent to my school so their families could say that their daughters had studied and were educated. As it was, none of us at the school went on to become teachers. We just got married.

I left school in September, two months before my wedding, and returned to my family home. Since Fourth Brother's return from Japan, our family fortune had improved considerably, and I did not think there was even need for me to get married so early. But, because the process had already been started a year or so earlier, there was no turning away from it.

Sixth Brother had been sent to Europe to oversee the purchase of my dowry. Chinese mahogany or ebony furniture would just not do, Fourth Brother had decided. All the homes and offices of the wealthiest Chinese in Shanghai—those who had made their fortunes dealing with foreigners in the treaty port—had Western-style furniture. Some of the pieces that Sixth Brother shipped back seemed straight out of the magazine pages that featured the craze for Western goods: a stuffed sofa, a matching armchair and ottoman, a display case with panes of glass, a bureau with five large drawers sized for big Westerners.

My dowry was so big that I could not arrive at Xiashi with it. In fact, there was so much furniture that it could not even fit on a train; Sixth Brother had to send it by barge from Shanghai. The transportation of the dowry was a formidable task. Once the furniture arrived at Xiashi, the pieces had to be carried through the streets of town to display the wealth of the new Hsü bride. Sixth Brother hired special servants for the task. They filled the chests with embroidered linen, and the glass-paneled cabinets with exquisite porcelain. They spread the new dining table with a fine linen cloth and set a meal for two with bowls, plates, teacups, spoons, chopsticks and even a flower vase holding a red blossom. Then, using the finest red silk, the servants bound the delicate place settings to the dining table so the bearers could carry the dowry through the streets in the manner that Hsü Chih-mo and I would use them.

No event this size had ever taken place in Xiashi, and the villagers lined the streets to marvel at my dowry as it was carried off the barge. Sixth Brother accompanied the furniture on its journey and became the first Chang family member to set foot in Xiashi. He sent a letter home telling Mama and Baba that the Hsü family was "a cow among the pigs." This meant that the Hsüs were indeed wealthy and respected among the villagers. We were greatly relieved. We had only known for certain that Hsü Chih-mo wrote a good essay!

When Sixth Brother returned to Nanchang, we learned even more about my new family: that the Hsüs had lived in Xiashi for several generations, and that my future father-in-law was one of the most successful in a line of entrepreneurs. The villagers called him "King of Xiashi" because he seemed to own everything: an electric power plant, a Chinese plum sauce factory, a silk material shop and a small bank in Shanghai. He also ran the town merchant guild. Unlike our family, the Hsüs had never suffered any financial turmoil.

As for my husband-to-be, Sixth Brother said with his eyes shining, he was brilliant. Hsü Chih-mo had a great future in front of him.

At the age of four, Hsü Chih-mo had started his education with a famous private tutor and shown early promise with the classics. At eleven, he had enrolled in a modern school that taught Western subjects. His classmates called him "Boy Wonder" and he became class president there by virtue of his academic record.

Hsü Chih-mo's will and spirit were excellent, Sixth Brother said. At fifteen, he was already like a grown-up scholar and the servants referred to him with great deference as "Shao Ye," their "Little Master." When he finished at the Hangzhou Middle School, his parents expected he would go to university for a few years in Beijing. Study overseas would then prepare him well for a career in the government or perhaps in his father's field of banking when he returned to China.

Of course, I was very happy to hear this news about Hsü Chih-mo. I thought I was marrying a man like my brothers, progressive yet traditional, with a strong set of values. I expected that he would go overseas to study, return to take a job in the ministry, and bring honor to his family.

I was supposed to arrive in Xiashi with a parade as big as the one for my dowry, but Sixth Brother thought it was too dangerous. The villagers had almost overturned the furniture and china, jostling one another for a look and touch. Ever practical, Baba and Fourth Brother decided that I should forgo the ceremonial entrance into Xiashi and arrive there anonymously. So, three days before the wedding, I boarded the train for Xiashi as if I were just leaving for a little holiday.

Traveling with an older married cousin, I was dressed in my everyday clothes. But still I felt the excited bride. Xiashi, the name of my new home, meant "Rocky Gorge." The town lay between the Western and Eastern Hills in Zhejiang Province. The smallest province of China, Zhejiang was one of the most densely populated and prosperous, home of the famous Longjing "Dragon Well" tea. It was said that the pure waters of this famed mountain site reached boiling point several degrees above normal and extracted the finest flavor from the Longjing tea leaves cultivated in the area.

I stared out the train window to imprint this journey in my memory. Terraced rice paddies with workers in pointed large-brimmed hats gave way to wheat and cotton fields rippling in shades of brown and purple. The sky appeared dappled through the leaves of mulberry trees that lined the edge of the railroad track; agile young girls picked the leaves to feed silkworms. Sticking my head out the window of the train, I was surprised to see beanstalks and melon vines growing in the banked dikes alongside the railroad track. The November air felt crisp and clean, and the countryside lay before me in prosperous beauty.

Arriving at Xiashi, we saw a huge crowd of villagers leaning up against the gates to the train station. With the wedding day so near, they had begun keeping a full-time vigil for me. My cousin and I darted for the nearest sedan chairs, regular green ones, and whispered our destination—the house the Hsüs had rented for the bride's family—to the front bearer. It was obvious he knew who we were from our destination. Nonetheless, he set off at a brisk pace without further comment.

The villagers had expected me to arrive in a sedan chair called the "flowered sedan chair." Reserved for the principal wife, it was covered in red satin and had thick curtains embroidered with butterflies for marital happiness, mandarin ducks for marital fidelity, and bats because the character for bats is a homonym for good fortune.

But when I drew aside the little curtain of my ordinary green sedan chair, I saw a small group of the country folk jogging alongside the bearers.

"It *is* her," several of them insisted.

"But it's not a red sedan chair," others answered breathlessly.

"Maybe she's trying to fool us," someone else said, and they all followed us from the train station anyway. This was the kind of country town I was moving to, where the villagers were the pigs and my husband's family the cow.

My cousin and I spent the night in the house reserved for the bride's family. We were alone except for the Hsü family servants. The following afternoon, two days before the wedding, my family arrived in Xiashi. Now the house was very crowded.

It was the tradition for the bride's family to invite the groom to dinner the evening before the wedding. Members of my family, not I, would give their final approval. Mama and Baba stayed upstairs to rest and assigned the older brothers to represent them at this dinner. Second Brother was studying in Berlin, so it was Fourth Brother and Sixth Brother, as chief hosts, who extended the invitation to Hsü Chih-mo.

As the hour drew near, my cousin and I hid behind the banister at the top of the staircase for our first glimpse of Hsü Chih-mo. We had seen only his picture, and there were tales of families who faked the groom's identity. I imagined the worst.

"If he has one eye and one leg," I said to my cousin, "I will not marry him; I will run away."

When Hsü Chih-mo arrived at the front door, I leaned forward to compare what I had seen in the picture. He seemed thinner and smaller and, somehow, very fragile.

"So, what do you think?" my cousin whispered. "Do you find him good-looking?"

I did not know what I considered handsome. "He's got two eyes and two legs," I answered. "So he's not terribly ugly."

We did not see any more of Hsü Chih-mo that evening, for he disappeared into the dining room. But I did see my brothers after the meal, which ended early, apparently, because Hsü Chih-mo had been too nervous to finish eating with them. The brothers said they liked him. They truly did, I could tell. Fourth Brother had finally met the man behind the essay and looked very satisfied and proud of his choice.

On your wedding day you will wear white because that is the Western color for brides. But in China the color white is only for mourning: a bride always wears red. I wore pink on my wedding, a combination of white and red, because Hsü Chih-mo had said that he wanted a modern bride. My dress was actually many layers of silk robes; the outer robe was pink with embroidered gold dragons. I also wore a headdress covered with jewels. In a step away from custom, Hsü Chih-mo would lift my heavy veil during the ceremonies, instead of waiting until the privacy of the bridal chamber.

My cousin coiled my hair into three small buns, the "three-flower" arrangement, and she carefully applied powder and rouge to my face. Her cool hands felt soothing against my skin. I had never tried to appear beautiful, and submitted myself curiously to the painting and tweezing, the penciling and plucking. Only after an hour did my cousin declare me "a plum blossom in the snow." I barely recognized myself in the mirror; I opened lips colored by vermillion and raised eyebrows etched in perfect arcs.

"No, no," my cousin corrected. "You must be withdrawn and grave." She instructed me to avert my gaze. I was not to look anyone in the eye, nor smile during the entire ceremony.

Mama and my cousin led me downstairs after they had placed the last of my wedding garments, an ornate headdress, atop my head. The rest of my family waited outside, Baba and my siblings dressed in their own silk robes. Mama lowered my veil just before I entered the red bridal sedan chair that would take me to the reception hall. Everything became pitch-black. Under the heavy weight of the headpiece, I nearly lost my balance and gasped in alarm.

"Shush," Mama murmured. "Walk tall today. Someone will always be here to guide you." Strong arms took hold of me and helped me into the sedan chair. A small band played somewhere behind me. I heard my female relatives breaking into the customary mock sobs. A firecracker exploded and startled me as I was hoisted up into my sedan chair. Settling myself into the seat, I tried not to tremble.

Because I wore the veil, I could not see, but I pictured our procession on the way to the reception hall. Four men—two displaying the banner of my family, two the banner of the Hsü family—led the parade. My sedan chair, with my brothers walking alongside, followed. Then came the green sedan chairs carrying the female members of my family. Finally, just before Hsü Chih-mo's procession, came the musicians underneath a red umbrella.

The sedan chair stopped as we reached the reception hall. My headdress rocked so precariously above me that I could keep my balance getting out of the chair only with help from my brothers. They led me into the wedding hall. I nearly retreated when I heard the din of the crowd; I knew our families had invited over three hundred guests.

As my eyes became accustomed to the darkness under the veil, I could make out shadows and movements. An escort led me slowly past the rows of guests to the front of the hall. A low table stood under a pool of light. Clumsily, I knelt in front of it. Next to me, a throat cleared nervously. Under the weight of the headpiece, I could not turn my head without effort, but I knew the noise came from Hsü Chih-mo kneeling next to me.

I had sneaked a peek at him the night before, but he had seen only the matchmaker's photograph of me. At the end of the ceremonies, as he reached for the edge of my bridal veil, I shook with fear and anticipation. The heavy veil had completely concealed my features. Now, exposed to his view, I could not meet his gaze, even though I had planned to disobey my cousin and stare directly at him. I had wanted to act as a modern girl, but I could not. Instead, I stared at his long, protruding chin. I wanted him to smile as he saw me for the first time. But his gaze remained sober.

At a Western wedding the bride and the groom are the honored people. They stand or sit down in one place, and guests go up to them in turn and pay their respects. At a Chinese wedding it is just the opposite. The guests are considered the honored people, and the bride and groom must kowtow to them. A full kowtow is like this: the person goes down on his knees, then puts his arms in front of him and touches his head to the ground, then after that stands up.

At our wedding Hsü Chih-mo and I stood in front of two red armchairs and kowtowed to each couple—names called off a long list—who sat in the armchairs. There were so many people we had to kowtow to that we could not do it all on our own; we actually each had a man behind us who helped push us down and pull us up. Push down and pull up; again and again for hours. I lost track of the faces. My legs ached so much that I could barely walk the whole next week.

In 1911 our country had changed from a monarchy to a republic, but the central government was weak and the land was controlled by local warlords. In 1915, the year of our wedding, skirmishes between warlords were commonplace. On our wedding day itself there was a minor fight in the Xiashi countryside, so that all the trains to Shanghai were canceled. No one could get back to the city. Hearing this news, many of the men left the wedding hall after the feast to contact their offices in Shanghai. Fourth Brother, Hsü Chih-mo's father and most of their friends were bankers. These men spent half the night telegraphing Shanghai to tell their assistants they would not be there the next day. The Hsüs had to book the town hotel and rent two other houses for all the overnight guests. Such big proceedings had never taken place before in Xiashi.

Now that most of the guests were spending the night, they stayed late and a lot of men crowded into the bridal room when the time came to "tease" the bride. This is a very old-fashioned custom: the bride sits in the middle of the room and people say mean things to her to test what kind of temper she has. I had to sit in the middle of the room and not say anything while Hsü Chih-mo's relatives and friends walked around me and poked fun at me. If I cried or laughed or spoke out, I would have been considered bad-tempered.

"Let's hear you sing," one said.

"Let's make her dance," another said.

"My, but you are ugly," one said. "Let us see those big feet," another said as he lifted my robe above my ankles so everyone could look and laugh. I did not say anything when he did that. I just let him do it. One of Hsü Chih-mo's friends even suggested they check to see the color of my underpants. Luckily, my brothers, hovering around me for protection, stopped them. Otherwise I would not have been able to object. This kind of teasing went on for many hours. Most of it Hsü Chih-mo did not see because he was in and out of the room joking with different people. Really, I think that everyone at my wedding had more fun there than I did.

Around four o'clock in the morning, all of a sudden, the guests left the bridal room. I was so tired that I just sat there. I must have been alone for only about five minutes when Hsü Chih-mo entered, followed by several servants. One servant pulled back the bedcovers and laid out a piece of white silk in the middle of the bed. I would have to display proof of my virginity on this cloth the following morning, my cousin had told me. The other servants helped me from my chair and led me toward the dressing table to prepare me for my wedding night.

In no time, I was ready. My hair, lightly scented with sandalwood, lay loose around my shoulders, held back from my face by two jade combs. I wore nothing except for a light red silk robe embroidered with mandarin ducks, the symbol of marital fidelity. When the servants left the room, I turned to Hsü Chih-mo.

He, too, had been undressed to only the lightest layer of silk and stood looking at me expectantly from across the room. Alone with him for the first time, I wanted so much to speak to him, to acknowledge my fate aloud. I wanted to say that I now belonged to the honorable Hsü family and hoped to serve them well. But the proper way was for him to address me first, so I waited.

I was young and scared. Maybe a modern girl would have spoken at that time and the couple would have started off right. But Hsü Chih-mo did not speak to me, so I did not answer him. And our silence toward each other began that night.

CHAPTER SEVEN

NEITHER THREE NOR FOUR

My mother told me that marriage was all about compromise, and that when I married a man I also married his family. My mother's in-laws lived in San Francisco, on the other side of America from her, but she felt their presence across her life. She sent them gifts regularly and reminded my father to call them at least twice a week. And if my father ever said a bad word about his own parents, my mother would reproach him or stay silent, never join in.

As much as I wanted to marry a Chinese to please my family, I feared that I would not meet the expectations of a daughter-in-law.

I worried that I would never be able to give birth to a son first as my mother did. My brother was the first grandson on both sides of the family, and everybody has more pictures of him than of any of the other grandchildren. Granted, my brother was the first grandchild to arrive for both families, but there are still far fewer pictures of the second grandchild, my female cousin, born only two years after my brother.

Secondly, ever since I was little, I had had too many preferences. Or, at least, certainly more than Mother, who never cared which restaurant we went out to. But I always liked the pizza topping at one place and the crust at another, and my mother used to say that I certainly had strong likes and dislikes for such a little girl. She worried for me being so picky.

Why worry? I used to think. I thought that my preferences gave me character. But when I visited Hong Kong as a twenty-one-year-old, I was told the same by my beautiful cousin, Pang Ru, who was married to a wealthy Chinese dentist.

"When you are with a man, sit very quiet and don't say anything," Pang Ru said, taking me out to tea at the finest hotel, the Shangri-la, so that we could talk seriously. "Let him show himself to you. Let him talk and then you decide."

I tried this advice one evening when I was having dinner with the parents of Adam, a Chinese man I once dated. Oddly enough, it felt good to play the quiet, gracious, potential daughter-in-law. I liked the fact that Adam's family and my own got along so well together. At the dinner table I picked out all the best pieces of chicken and fish and, using the back end of my chopsticks courteously, I served Adam's parents, Adam, and finally myself.

Then Adam's father said, commenting in general about the wife of his other son, "I never say much to my daughter-in-law. The father-in-law should not get too close to the daughter-in-law."

When I heard that I nearly choked on my food. It was one thing for me to play at being the subservient daughter-in-law and future wife, quite another for the role to be so absolutely defined.

Another time, years later, I told what I thought was a funny story about my future in-laws' idiosyncrasies to my parents. Afterward my father said, "If you are going to marry this man, never say an unkind word about your in-laws, especially in front of me. It is very poor manners and let's not allow this to happen again."

I do not know what your mother has told you about marriage, but when I married, my mother gave me only two pieces of advice.

The first was that, once I entered the Hsü household, I must never say no, only yes.

The second was that, no matter what ever happened between my husband and me, I had to treat my in-laws the same. To show my respect, I had to rise each morning before they did and bid them "Good morning"—this was the only time I could speak before being spoken to—and in the evening I had to wait until they had given me leave before I could retire.

Mama called these "the obligatory morning and evening greetings." I had to wake up early, wash my face, comb my hair, attire myself in formal clothing and greet my in-laws at the approved time every day. Throughout the day, I was not to show myself to them in anything but the most correct attire, and never with my hair down, which was considered wild.

That was the most Mama ever told me. In those days no one talked about sex or relationships. Not like these days, where everything is talked about. You young people learn so much from television or magazines. The only way I ever learned about menstruation, for instance, was by accident, from the mentally retarded servant back in Jiading who sewed the cloth shoes. She used to leave all her menstruation cloths around the yard for the dogs and chickens to sniff at, or else wave them around the yard for everyone to see. Crazy, but that was how I found out; my mother did not tell me.

Still, the advice she did give me ended up being very sound, and I tell it to you now that you are entering marrying years. In the

Chinese household the parents rule. Therefore a woman's relationship with her in-laws, especially her mother-in-law, is often more important than her relationship with her husband. Because you are Chinese and will marry a Chinese, I must correct two bad habits of yours. I notice sometimes when I am at your house and you come to say good night to me you turn away before I tell you that you may go. This is very bad; you must change this before you marry.

Another habit is this American way of saying, "I'm tired," when people ask how you are. Never in my life have I said I was tired. I remember my first morning at the Hsü house, I had barely slept and I was aching all over from kowtowing and everything, but I never thought that I was tired and could not get up to prepare myself for my in-laws. I always knew my duties to my father-in-law, Lao Ye, and my mother-in-law, Lao Taitai.

In the beginning, of course, it was difficult to know how to please them. The Chinese do not say yes or no or this or that or tell you straight out, so sometimes I had to guess. For instance, my mother-in-law rarely entered the kitchen. There were a lot of servants and, unlike Baba, my father-in-law was not very particular about his food. So once, when Lao Taitai went into the kitchen, I was so surprised I stood by her side doing nothing. One of the old servants who had been in the house for years and knew how to wait on Lao Taitai quickly handed me a fan and said with pity in his voice, "You might as well make yourself useful and keep your mother-in-law cool while she cooks."

Later I learned little things. One of the local country customs during the New Year, Fifth Moon and Moon Festival holidays was to exchange gifts with everyone in an elaborate but very silly manner. This was the system: someone would send us four gifts and we would say, "Oh, four gifts is much too generous," and keep only two gifts, sending back the other two. Then we would send out four gifts and they would send us back two. Lao Taitai hated to waste money, so we would set aside gifts in piles of two and wait for two more gifts—either our own returned or two others from someone else—so we could send out another grouping of four. The process was complicated because we had to make sure we did not repeat gifts with the same or related people. We were forever adjusting and worrying about our different piles of presents.

On a whim while I was home visiting my family, I decided to surprise my mother-in-law and buy the presents for the relatives and villagers all at once. My father-in-law gave me ten or twenty yuan a month which I never spent, so I used forty yuan and shopped all afternoon in Shanghai for hams and ducks and other delicacies.

When I returned to Xiashi at the end of my visit home, I was laden with gifts. Lao Taitai asked me how much everything had cost.

"Twenty yuan," I lied.

Lao Taitai smiled. "That's not bad."

"Good," I said. "Let's just send out four gifts to each family directly, and finish everything."

In these small ways, I tried to please Lao Taitai.

I never learned to please my husband as I did my in-laws, although in bed, strangely enough, we became husband and wife together very naturally. Even that first time on our wedding night. I think that is because we were two young people. Also, before then, neither of us knew anything about what forms the male and female bodies. So we had to learn from each other. But almost immediately I began to get caught up taking care of the in-laws. And in the countryside, women were not allowed to set foot outside of the compound. So, when Hsü Chih-mo would leave in the mornings, I was not allowed to go along with him. Several weeks after our marriage, Hsü Chih-mo left to go study, first at Beiyang University in Tianjin and then at Beijing University in the capital. So you see, this is very sad: from the beginning I did not get to know my husband.

Beijing University was the most famous university at the time, a place run mainly by returned students—those who had studied in the West and brought their learning back to China. In letters home to his parents, Hsü Chih-mo told us of his exciting life. At the university, Second Brother introduced him to Liang Qichao, the famous reformer, who took on Hsü Chih-mo as a disciple.

Hsü Chih-mo also met Hu Shi, who was famous for an article in the *New Youth* magazine calling for the end of the old literature in classical Chinese and for a new literature in vernacular language that reflected popular sentiment. When Hsü Chih-mo became a poet after studying in the West, he used this vernacular language and brought it to new levels of expression.

Listening to Lao Ye read aloud Hsü Chih-mo's letters, I envied my husband's freedom. At first I also thought that I would go back to school. I wrote to the teacher's college in Suzhou to ask if I might return. The officials told me that I would have to repeat the previous year because I had already missed a term. This meant that I would not finish for another two years. I did not think that I could leave my in-laws for so long at the beginning of my marriage. I was Hsü Chih-mo's wife, the daughter-in-law of the richest family in town. Already the villagers thought me too modern. They laughed at my big feet. When I went home to Shanghai almost every month because I was lonesome, the villagers asked, "Why does this daughter-in-law go to Shanghai so often? The Hsü father has business in the city, but why does the daughter-in-law go so frequently? Does she have a bad temper? Not get along with Lao Taitai? Big feet, big temper," the villagers snickered.

Lao Ye, who did business with everyone, said that such talk

was bad and that I should refrain from leaving town so often. I came from the city and was not used to sitting on the compound all day, prohibited from shopping on my own or visiting friends and relatives. But I obeyed. And I knew that boarding school was out of the question. Still, though, can you imagine marrying at age fifteen and never studying anymore? Never knowing anything else? Later, when I was vice-president of the Shanghai Women's Savings Bank, I had a tutor come to the office because I thought, I know so little. To stop learning at age fifteen is difficult.

I had nothing to do all day except stay at home with Lao Taitai. We would sit for hours in the women's quarters sewing shoes for the family. Back home in Jiading, we had that crazy servant who used to make them all. But here, even though we were rich, we made them ourselves. To Lao Taitai, our slippers were special. After we had stitched a thick sole to coarse black fabric to form the shoe, we would thread a fine needle with pure silk to create the delicate embroidery that embellished the toe of each slipper. There was the multilayered "cumulus cloud pattern" that shimmered as Lao Taitai walked. Or the "longevity" character that made a bold statement with each step. For Lao Taitai's tiny slippers, I embroidered small delicate stitches; for my own, I sewed wild and careless ones because it did not matter to me what I wore. I was never allowed out anyway. I never even saw the places that the Hsüs owned until after I came back from Europe. By then, the customs had loosened. And I had lived in the West for five years and did not care what the villagers thought.

The servants said Lao Ye was a smart one: he knew how to hold on to his money. He did not keep concubines at the house. Instead, he had girlfriends in town, so many he could not choose among them. There was one for each direction: north, south, east, west. I learned these facts the many nights I waited up late for Lao Ye, often until two or three in the evening. As Mama had instructed, I greeted my in-laws first thing in the morning and last thing in the evening. How difficult this was for me! Lao Taitai was an early riser, and Lao Ye a late sleeper.

In the teahouses where Lao Ye spent his evenings, the servants said, lily-footed ladies danced on tables and lured men with glimpses of their insteps barely covered by wrappings and dainty silk slippers. The mincing gait of these maidens, who could not stray beyond the limits of their rooms, bewitched men, young and old alike. He who beat out all others in a drinking game downed his last from one tiny embroidered slipper whose owner lay waiting for him on the top floor of the teahouse. In the intimacy of her chambers she would unravel the bindings of her feet and reveal them to him. That evening, in a final moment of passion, he would lift her tiny unwrapped feet to his shoulders and thrust them into his mouth to suck.

These were the stories of tiny feet I heard from the servants, and they filled my ears. Bound feet were a woman's prized possessions, part of her dowry, gifts from a wealthy father to be presented to the worthy man. Once, in the old times, a man walking down the streets of the village had briefly fondled the bound foot of a young maiden riding by on horseback. Her reputation had almost been dishonored.

I listened so closely to tales of small feet that my own big feet lost their magic for me. I had thought they made me modern, but instead they became my enemy. They could not walk the village streets, they could not make me educated. Nor could they make my husband care for me.

When Hsü Chih-mo came home during the holidays, he ignored me except for the most basic of marital duties. Even then, he was only obeying his parents' wishes for a grandson. I did not understand why he behaved this way, especially since my brothers were his friends; he obviously approved of my family. So why did he treat me so poorly?

Sometimes I sat with him, sewing while he read, stretched out in a long chair in the courtyard. "Fetch me this," he would say to one servant. "Scratch here," he would say to another. But he never spoke to me. I was too young to know how to react. I kept the silence. If he did not wish to speak to me, I thought, I could be silent for days. What had I expected from marriage? Not love, not yet at least. Not romance, but certainly more than what I had: indifference. Hsü Chih-mo never looked at me, only through me, as if I did not exist. All my life I had lived with educated men like him—my father and brothers—and they had not treated me like this. Only my husband.

Some mornings, especially when the weather was good, Hsü Chih-mo would disappear without saying a word. I would learn from a servant that he had taken a sedan chair up to the family's house in the Eastern Hills. I had never been up there but knew that the stone figure of a woman could be seen from the peak of the Eastern Hills. According to local legend, a woman climbed a lookout hill to scan the sea when her trader husband failed to return home. She waited so long for him that at last her weeping body turned to solid rock, and the villagers named the peak Wangfushan, the "Husband-Gazing Hill." So I suppose I was up there in the mountains in spirit.

And now I understood what my amah had meant about being "neither three nor four." I was supposed to be a modern girl with big feet, but Hsü Chih-mo treated me as though I had bound feet. He thought me old-fashioned and uneducated, and did not care for me. Yet I was not traditional enough for Lao Taitai. With her bound feet, she was content to spend every day in the female quarters; I wanted to explore the streets of Xiashi. After all the hopes of my amah and Mama, I was neither a sister of the sun as Mama had dreamed I would be, nor a sister of the moon as my amah had wanted me to be.

Lao Taitai always watched me closely during the weeks after Hsü Chih-mo's visits home. One day, when I had no appetite at lunch, she looked intently at me and said with certainty in her voice, "You are expecting a child."

How strange that she knew before me, but as it turned out, she was correct. I felt quite ill for the first three months. But beginning the fourth month, when I could feel the child move, I began to hope that I carried a boy.

I already told you that a woman is nothing in China. Now I will tell you why. People pass from the Light World to the Shadow World when they die. The Shadow World is female, Yin, the Negative Essence, the moon, and all things passive and deep. The Light World is male, Yang, Positive Essence, the sun, and all things strong and high.

You might think it unfair, but only males—sons, grandsons, great-grandsons and all in unending succession—have the proper elements of the Light World in order to care for ancestors in the Shadow World. Caring correctly for the ancestors and maintaining the balance between the worlds is very important. Otherwise, the dead will leave the Shadow World and invade the Light World as lonely ghosts. We women can only assure our places in both the Light World and the Shadow World by providing male descendants for our husbands' families.

So this is why the Chinese like boys, especially the first child. I remember hearing of a concubine in the countryside who worried so much about her position in the household after giving birth to a girl, she swore the midwife to secrecy and dressed the daughter like a boy for fifteen years, until it could no longer be concealed. Can you imagine that! I too wanted a son, but as my pregnancy wore on, I swore to myself that if the baby was a daughter I would not treat her that way. I would not abandon her in the fields with her *bazi* pinned to her blankets so that whoever found her could marry her off immediately as a child bride. I would not bind her feet and restrict her from studying.

As was the custom of the bride's mother, Mama came to visit me in my last weeks of term. Mama had not come to Xiashi since the wedding. These were her only occasions to come. She arrived at my bedside with a bundle of baby clothes. With a quick motion, I shook the bundle across the bed, trying to make the bundle open by itself and send the clothes flying across the bed. It did not open.

"Ah well," Mama said, shaking her head, "you will be a long time in labor."

I groaned. "You didn't tie it properly. Here, let me see."

"Now don't argue," Mama said. And she motioned for the servant to bring a tray over to my bed. On the tray was a specially prepared bowl of rice. Underneath the rice, at the bottom of the bowl, Mama had placed meatballs and hard-boiled eggs alternating in a round.

I took the pair of chopsticks Mama handed me and stabbed at the bottom of the bowl. I pulled up a meatball at the end of my chopstick.

Mama wrinkled her face. "Humph, only a girl, not a boy."

I looked up at her. "If you had given me ordinary bamboo chopsticks, it might have been good. But you gave me the ivory chopsticks and they slipped to the meatball instead of the egg."

"Don't argue," Mama said. "Accept your fate. It will be a girl."

Yu-i's mother, striking an aristocratic pose.

Yu-i's father, a respected doctor who ruled the household with a firm hand.

Yu-i with her brothers and sisters, gathered in Shanghai in 1927 for their parents' funeral. Seated, from left, First and Fourth Sisters, and Yu-i. Standing, Third Sister and two sisters-in-law. Seated, from left, First, Second, Eighth, Fifth and Third Brothers. Standing, Seventh, Fourth and Sixth Brothers.

Yu-i and Hsü Chih-mo, looking stylish in their first photograph taken together in the West, 1921. They divorced the following year.

At left, Yu-i's First Sister, whose feet were bound, and her husband, with Yu-i's in-laws, vacationing together in Hangzhou. First Sister grew so close with the in-laws that they once said they wished that First Sister had married their son, Hsü Chih-mo.

Yu-i's Second Brother, Chang Chia-sen, and Hsü Chih-mo. The date of the photograph is unknown, but Yu-i believed that her brother would not have thought it proper to pose with Hsü Chih-mo after the divorce.

Yu-i in Germany, 1924. She said that a lady always wore a hat in the streets, or risked being mistaken for a servant.

From left, Second Brother, Mrs. Liu, Yu-i (with child) and Mr. Liu. The Lius, both students at the University of Paris, were kind enough to take in a pregnant Yu-i after Hsü Chih-mo left her.

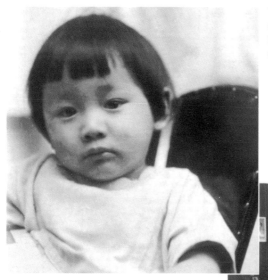

Yu-i's second son, Peter, at age two, a year before his death in 1925. Born in Berlin, he met his father only once.

Dora Berger, Yu-i's only friend in Berlin, loved Peter so much she kept his photograph hanging over her desk after his death.

Yu-i posing with her mother and her sisters shortly after her return from Germany. Notice her decidedly Western dress and striped hat in contrast to her traditional sisters.

Yu-i's Eighth Brother—my grandfather, Chang Chia-Chu—dressed up to attend Hsü Chih-mo's second wedding. He was so devoted to Hsü Chih-mo that he requested one of Hsü Chih-mo's poems read at his own funeral.

Eighteen-year-old Yu-i with her first son, the pride of the Hsü family.

Yu-i's first son, Hsü Chi-kai, who the family called A-huan, meaning "Little Happiness," with his paternal grandmother outside the Hsü family home in Xiashi.

Yu-i with a teenage A-huan. She raised her son on her own after returning from Germany in 1926.

一九四五年攝於紐約

My grandfather, Chang Chia-chu (standing), surrounded by Second and Fourth Brothers, Chang Chia-sen and Chang Chia-ao, on a visit to America in 1945. Eventually, they all settled in Northern California.

Yu-i surrounded by her grandchildren in front of the house on Avenue Hague, Shanghai. From left, Margaret, Angela, Fern and Tony.

My family and I in Hamden, Connecticut, 1991. From left, my father, sister, brother, me and my mother. Seated on my brother's lap is the family dog, Guilin, named after a city in China famous for peaked mountains that line the River Li.

Yu-i and me in her New York City apartment, Christmas, 1986

Yu-i in Shanghai, about 1937. As vice president of the Shanghai Women's Savings Bank, she donned her black silk cheongsam for this formal portrait.

"I am not arguing," I persisted. "I am just saying that the ivory is too slick. Let's wait and see. We'll see if it's not a boy."

I fainted during my labor, and no one even roused me. They did not bother. I only woke because I had given birth to a son and the midwife screamed, "It's a boy!" Usually, in the old days, country people did not do that. They did not want the gods to know that a boy had been born; otherwise, the gods would take him.

My in-laws were thrilled. They passed out red-dyed eggs to announce the arrival of the new Hsü heir. Lying in bed, listening to their celebrations, I felt so relieved. What a blessing to bring a healthy son into the world! I cherished him at first sight and prayed that in my old age I would long enjoy his filial devotion.

Now that the issue of the heir was settled, Hsü Chih-mo was free to travel overseas. That summer of 1918, shortly after our son's birth, he left to study banking and sociology at Clark University, in Worcester, Massachusetts. Like most new fathers, he seemed proud and somewhat in awe of his son. Toward me, however, Hsü Chih-mo remained the same. When I bade him goodbye, he seemed already gone. Perhaps he had never been there.

CHAPTER EIGHT

ACCORDING TO
YOUR WISHES

O ne historian's account suggests that Hsü Chih-mo was like other young men of his social class when he left China for the West. Twenty-two years old, he was looking for a way to help his country. He intended to go to the West and return to China prepared to take over his family business or join the government bureaucracy. But, according to the historian, Hsü Chih-mo's journey to the West infused him with a desire to change his ways. He embraced what he considered to be the essence of the West and devoted himself to becoming a living embodiment of those virtues and traits that he most admired in the West: love, passion, honesty.

Often I asked Yu-i, "But weren't you angry at Hsü Chih-mo?"

I know that I was torn. I hated the way Hsü Chih-mo treated Yu-i, but despite myself I could not help but feel tremendous admiration for him and his work. He belonged to an elite brotherhood, a transitional generation of scholars who changed China. As the first of my family born in the States, I hoped to be like him, one infused with both Western and Eastern learning.

Yu-i, though, would not admit her feelings, I assumed, because a proper Chinese woman is not supposed to feel animosity.

When Hsü Chih-mo left for the United States, his ambition was to go into finance, to become, as he put it, the Alexander Hamilton of China. During this period he even adopted the Western name Hamilton for himself. His self-imposed schedule at Clark University shows him to be infused with ambition and a sense of national duty.

> *Get up at six, morning meeting [with four Chinese roommates] at seven (to stimulate our sense of national shame); in the evening, sing the national anthem and go to bed at ten-thirty. During the day, besides studying diligently, do exercises, run, and read newspapers.*

Hsü Chih-mo's desire to "stimulate national shame" or, in other words, to rally himself and his peers to action interested me. I had read about China's sense of national shame in my history books and learned the historical theory why Communism succeeded in China: Confucianism failed to protect the nation against western imperialism. Having grown up Chinese in America, and gotten teased for my race, I felt familiar with the concept of shame, but wondered how it would have felt to be like Hsü Chih-mo, so much a part of a people that I could envision myself a leading voice of my generation.

After graduating with high honors from Clark University, Hsü Chih-mo transferred to Columbia University in 1919 to study political science. However, finding America incompatible with his temperament, he abandoned his studies and moved abruptly to England in 1920. "It was a time," he wrote, "when I was feeling deeply depressed and searching for new directions." Shortly afterward, he developed his personal credo of love, which was to affect Yu-i so strongly.

The Hsü family doted upon my son, Hsü Chi-kai, from birth. Wrapped in swaddling clothes of the finest cotton, he never cried for more than a few moments until a servant or wet nurse soothed him, and his first toy, a small carved ivory scepter called a *ruyi*, meant "according to your wishes." His grandparents declared their only grandchild more precious to them than all the immense wealth in the world and, from token donations of one hundred family members, commissioned for Hsü Chi-kai a tiny iron lock. This "Hundred Family Lock," which hung around his neck on a gold chain, was meant to "lock" Hsü Chi-kai into life with the blessings of one hundred loved ones, and show the joy that he brought to the family.

We named him Chi-kai, which means "fine iron," after the metal that symbolizes strength, integrity, determination and justice. His inquisitive nature delighted everyone in the household, and soon A-huan, meaning "happiness," became his nickname. Grandmother Hsü insisted that we visit her with him often, and Lao Taitai turned from stitching shoes every day to infant clothes.

Although I had been fairly weak after the birth, I recovered quickly and looked forward to caring for my son. But I soon discovered that, like almost all my social behavior in the Hsü household, my role as mother was strictly prescribed. A-huan belonged to the Hsü family: Grandmother Hsü, Lao Ye and Lao Taitai would supervise his upbringing. I was allowed to tend to my son only occasionally. When I did hold him, the in-laws corrected me; when I did bathe him, the nursemaid hovered. At night a wet nurse slept on the floor alongside his crib.

"Never say no, only yes," Mama had told me. So I did not object to my in-laws' ways. But now I see all that I relinquished in order to please my in-laws: walks outside, my schooling, and even my child. I am so fortunate that my son and daughter-in-law live near me now, and we are able to see each other often. I did not get to care for A-huan the way a mother should for a son the first seven years of his life.

On the hundredth day after A-huan's birth, a servant placed before my son a tray that held a tailor's ruler, a small abacus, one of Hsü Chih-mo's calligraphy brushes and some coins. We all gathered around A-huan to see which object he would grasp first and thereby indicate the direction of his future. First, A-huan stared at the entire tray with wonder, his eyes barely distinguishing among the various things. Then he became transfixed in turn by the abacus, the tool of the merchant, and the ruler, the tool of the craftsman. Finally, his eyes fastened on one item in the center of the tray, and after a moment of apparent fascination, he reached for the object: Hsü Chih-mo's calligraphy brush.

What a clever boy! I was so proud. This meant that my son showed promise of becoming a scholar like Hsü Chih-mo and my brothers.

Lao Ye swung A-huan up in the air with sudden exuberance. "Another scholar! Our grandson will use the iron pen!" he boasted to Lao Taitai, drawing from a line often used in important government proclamations: "The iron pen changes not." Lao Ye was expressing his hope that A-huan, formally named after the metal iron, would one day write government decrees.

A few months later, in the fall of 1918, we celebrated again when the First World War came to a close. Second Brother, who had been managing an independent newspaper in Shanghai since his return from Germany, intended to travel with Liang Qichao and others as an unofficial delegation to the Peace Conference in 1919. I saw Second Brother shortly before he left, when I was home visiting my parents.

"When will you join Hsü Chih-mo in the West?" Second Brother wanted to know.

I looked at him in surprise. Hsü Chih-mo had been in America for half a year, and I had not considered joining him because I thought it was my duty to stay with my in-laws.

"You have fulfilled your duty to the Hsü family," Second Brother said as if he heard my thoughts. "Now you should go be with your husband. You could even study in the West."

Study in the West like a modern woman? Learn a foreign language like Hsü Chih-mo and my brothers? The idea intrigued me. Then I remembered my in-laws. Would the Hsüs let me go to America? Would they pay for my studies? I told Second Brother that the Hsüs probably would only let me go if Hsü Chih-mo sent for me; they hated to refuse their son.

"Hsü Chih-mo will send for you," Second Brother assured me. "He would want you to understand the West."

Since my brother was good friends with Hsü Chih-mo, I believed him and returned to Xiashi excited at the prospect. I had lived with the Hsüs for almost four years now, and with Hsü Chih-mo, maybe only four months during his holidays. I longed to be able to speak with Hsü Chih-mo as freely as I did with my brothers. I wanted to help him, contribute to his success and honor. In one daydream I saw the two of us as companions in a simple home, he studying as I prepared a meal for two. In another, I pictured myself in Western dress holding books and walking alongside Hsü

Chih-mo on the way to class, like my schooldays with First Sister at the Teachers' College Preparatory School.

Now, each time Hsü Chih-mo's letters were read aloud, I waited for him to mention me. Hsü Chih-mo always addressed letters to his parents and asked about A-huan and me at the end. This was considered very filial: a husband and wife were supposed to act distant with each other in front of the in-laws. Once Hsü Chih-mo asked me to follow A-huan around the entire day and write down everything that he said or did. Another time he asked to see A-huan's drawings and beginning attempts at calligraphy. But still he did not send for us.

In the spring of 1919, China learned the terms of the peace treaty negotiated in Paris: as part of some secret pact among the Allies, Shandong Province, the birthplace of Confucius, would be given to Japan. Years of intense resentment against imperialistic foreign powers were touched off by this show of the Allies' treachery. On Tiananmen Square in Beijing on May 4, 1919, some three thousand students staged a mass demonstration, demanding that the government refuse the terms of the treaty. "Down with imperialism! Return Shandong to us!" "Boycott Japanese goods!" they shouted.

The following day a general protest strike was organized, and students in cities across the country joined in demonstrations of their own. The show of patriotism swept over the country. Thousands of workers met to discuss the boycott of Japanese goods. On June 5, some 20,000 workers in Shanghai called a strike that affected many enterprises including Japanese-owned cotton mills.

Lao Ye closed up some of the shops in Shanghai temporarily

and stayed home in Xiashi reading newspaper reports. The government ultimately released the arrested students, and China did not accept the peace treaty. The students and workers were victorious.

Second Brother returned from Europe excited at the outcome of the demonstrations. Then he asked me, "Has Hsü Chih-mo sent for you yet?"

I shook my head.

"Something must be wrong that he has not sent for you this long," he said.

When Second Brother said these words, I was suddenly reminded of something that Hsü Chih-mo had said to me about a year before I became pregnant. He said a change was sweeping over China that meant freedom, no more slavery to ancient customs. Pacing the room like a caged animal, he said that he would challenge these traditions that kept him from acting on his own true feelings: he would be the first man in China to get a divorce.

I remember being surprised at his comment, but not worried or upset. As a child, the only divorces I had ever heard of occurred when the woman was unfaithful, or jealous, or did not serve the family well. Of course I had not done that. Also, I had heard that a woman would be so disgraced by divorce, her family would not want her back, so she had only three choices: prostitution, the nunnery, or suicide. I could not believe that Hsü Chih-mo would force me into these situations. I knew Hsü Chih-mo's background and his family.

So I did not listen closely or take Hsü Chih-mo's words about divorce seriously. I thought he was just preparing to leave for the West and playing at being Western.

But at Second Brother's comment, I heard Hsü Chih-mo's remark again. The student demonstrations had shown me that Hsü Chih-mo was right: a movement was sweeping across the country. I thought perhaps one of the reasons Hsü Chih-mo was not sending for me was because he did not think that I wanted to go to the West; he did not think he could take the country bumpkin out of the country.

I had never dared ask my in-laws if I could travel overseas. Second Brother said he would ask Lao Ye for me. Second Brother and Lao Ye often met for tea when Lao Ye was in Shanghai on business. The next time they saw each other, Second Brother said, "Hsü Chih-mo and Yu-i will grow apart in mind if Hsü Chih-mo continues to study abroad and Yu-i stays in Xiashi."

"She keeps Lao Taitai company. She has to care for the baby," Lao Ye replied.

The Hsüs were very old-fashioned and did not want me to travel overseas. They believed that I belonged in the home. They believed in the old saying that a girl's ignorance is her virtue. Of course, they had some reason to their thinking. A girl who does not know anything and does not want to know anything is so much more manageable than one who is always learning and always wants to know more. But this is old thinking. The family did not understand that it would have been better for their grandson if I knew something. If I learned, then I could pass that on to my child, be a better mother.

While the family deliberated on whether or not I should go to the West, I begged Lao Ye to hire a tutor for me. Lao Ye's brother had several unmarried daughters who were willing to learn. It was with these three younger girls that I attended classes. By the time the family decided that I would be allowed to join Hsü Chih-mo, I had been studying for about a year, but the decision to let me go had nothing to do with furthering my studies. I think that the in-laws decided to send me because they suspected something was wrong with Hsü Chih-mo. He had surprised everyone by leaving his Ph.D.

studies at Columbia and heading for Europe. His letters indicated that he was feeling restless and depressed. His parents were worried about him.

I was happy to get my wish, even though it was decided that I would leave my two-year-old son behind with my in-laws. Also, the Hsüs would only let me travel with a family. A man alone would not have been right, but a woman alone would have been dangerous. Luckily, a Chinese family from the Spanish consulate—husband, wife and two children—was bound for Marseilles. So we traveled over together on the same steamer. I did not tend to the children at all, just sat in my own compartment.

At night on the ship I lay in bed thinking how I would act when I first met Hsü Chih-mo. I remembered the long silences with him—how he called me a "country bumpkin" from the beginning—and my heart filled with heaviness. I had lived with my husband's family for five years now, but I did not know my husband. I tried to tell myself that we had not grown too far apart. Aboard the ship, I thought how hard I had worked with the tutor and hoped Hsü Chih-mo would notice how much more educated I was now. And I wanted to study hard in the West, to learn English.

When the other steamship passengers learned that I was journeying abroad to join my husband, they told me I was very lucky. How wonderful for your husband to send for you, they said. I said nothing, because I knew that Hsü Chih-mo had not sent for me; I was being sent. I think my in-laws had agreed to let me go just to remind Hsü Chih-mo of his duties to his family in China.

Three weeks later, when the boat finally made its way in to the Marseilles pier, I leaned forward on deck and waited impatiently for the landing. And then I saw Hsü Chih-mo among the onlookers, and in that precise second my heart froze. He was dressed in a long, narrow, black wool coat with a white silk scarf around his neck. I had never seen him in Western clothes but knew it was he. His carriage was unmistakable, so easy to spot, the only one in the crowd of receivers who looked as though he did not want to be there. It had been so long since we had been together that I had almost forgotten how he always looked through me like that, directly beyond me as if I did not exist.

After being at sea for three weeks, I felt the land shaking beneath my feet, but nothing else had changed. By the time I stood opposite Hsü Chih-mo, I had calmed everything in my face—the eagerness, the happiness, the hope. At that moment I hated Hsü Chih-mo for reducing me to this flatness, this stiffness. Things had always been like this with him. How could I have thought we would have things to say to each other, that he might try to make me feel a part of his world?

He wanted to see Paris, he said, so we went directly from the port to the train station. We spoke very little to each other even on the train ride—maybe a few words about my trip and the family back home. One of the first stops upon our arrival in Paris was a department store where he and the saleslady picked out some foreign clothes for me. What I had chosen from the Xiashi merchants and laid out to wear with great care in my ship cabin the night before was all wrong.

I do not know what language Hsü Chih-mo spoke—it must have been French although I didn't think he knew it—but he chattered away with the saleslady choosing clothes for me. No, he said, shaking his head and looking me up and down coldly, not that dress. How about that one? And he held it against me, touching me for the first time since my arrival. When I saw myself in the mirror with the long slim dress, felt the sensation of stockings on my legs and the heavy tightness of the leather shoes, I did not know myself. We bought a hat, too, to go with the outfit, and that first day, with my new clothes on, we went to have our pictures taken. We sent these pictures to Lao Ye and Lao Taitai to show them how the two of us were together and living well in this strange land.

From Paris, we flew to London in a plane so small I had to sit across from him, both knees straddled with his. I had never before been in a plane and was sick in a paper bag. I was not scared; the air was bad and the flight bumpy. As I retched, Hsü Chih-mo turned away from me and shook his head in disgust. "What a country bumpkin you are," he said.

Shortly afterward, though, he too fell sick in a bag. I said, softly because the malice was petty and spoke for itself, "Oh, I see you too are a country bumpkin."

Two of Hsü Chih-mo's friends met us at the London airport. Apparently, daily service between Paris and London had begun only a year before, and his friends asked us eagerly how the flight was. Hsü Chih-mo was suddenly alive, chattering away excitedly in English. They were Chinese, the friends, and we could have all spoken Chinese. But Hsü Chih-mo did not want to do that, and they made an exclusive threesome. One friend kept stopping to hike up his pants every minute, the other wrinkled half his face in a nervous twitch all the time.

"So these are your friends," I said to Hsü Chih-mo when we were alone. But he gave me another empty look and turned away.

In London we stayed at a club that seemed to be the place for all the Chinese in the city. There were a lot of us there during that time. Everyone knew everyone else and was here for one reason or another to study. Those who knew Hsü Chih-mo raised their eyes when they saw me, seemingly surprised. Hsü Chih-mo had been living alone in London for a year already, taking courses at the London School of Economics.

We spoke Chinese with one another and ate Chinese food, and even Hsü Chih-mo seemed to shed his foreign ways. He sipped tea and sometimes changed into a long Manchu robe for dinner downstairs, where we ate with all the other Chinese. Maybe he preferred wearing Chinese clothes when eating Chinese food, I do not know.

Next to the dining room was a lounge. After dinner everyone went there and talked about government and politics, poetry and literature. Quite a few women were there too. I did not say much but sat there listening. A few people knew of and admired my Second and Fourth Brothers, and they told me so.

One man asked me where I had just come from and, when I told him Xiashi, he asked me which family. I told him the Hsü family.

"Oh," he said, "there is a man there named Hsü Shen-ju."

"Yes," I said, "that is my father-in-law."

"Oh," he said again. "That is a very rich family, one of the richest in the province."

This was a strange thing for him to say, because in China it was considered very bad manners to talk about money. I did not know how to respond.

"That may be so," I finally said after a long pause. "But we young people do not meddle in the business affairs."

I could have acted differently in the West from the beginning, I know. I could have walked on the streets, tried to see things on my own. But I did not. To this day, I do not know why I did nothing except wait for Hsü Chih-mo. It did not even occur to me then that I could have been independent.

All the time, he went about his business as if I were not there.

He dashed in and out, making arrangements. He was to be a special student in literature at Cambridge University, King's College, and went about planning a move to Cambridge. There were lodgings to rent and travel arrangements to make. Hsü Chih-mo told me just to stay in the room and let him be. So I sat in the Chinese club in the middle of London and felt lost because all the other Chinese, even the women, had errands to run or studies to complete. I had nothing to do. Hsü Chih-mo returned to the room at intervals only to leave again, seemingly surprised each time to find me still there. Where would I have gone, I thought in reply, but perhaps he believed it possible to will my disappearance each time he left me behind.

At first I thought it was my helplessness that repelled Hsü Chih-mo. But there was more. Like the starched shirts with pointed collars and three-button woolen jackets he now donned each morning, Hsü Chih-mo was foreign. He was alien to me. He punctuated his speech with a lighted cigarette instead of a folded fan, and drank his tea thick and pale with sugar and milk.

He was truly in a different world, chattering away in English to a foreigner named Goldsworthy Lowes Dickinson whom he brought back to the room just once. Hsü Chih-mo called Dickinson "Goldie," and I understood that he had been the one who arranged for Hsü Chih-mo to study at Cambridge University. Hsü Chih-mo was always happy with his friends, but from just one meeting, seeing the two of them together, I could tell that Hsü Chih-mo was particularly fond of Dickinson. I watched his animated body movements and listened to the respect in his voice. When Hsü Chih-mo returned to our room after sending Dickinson back home, I saw his utter disdain for me.

I revolted Hsü Chih-mo. He was never abusive, but usually by the evening he was not happy that I was there. When the sun shone and he did not have to be with me much, he was neutral, even pleasant toward me. Then, inevitably, with dusk, a certain melancholy seemed to fall over him, and by evening's end, when he bade his friends good night, it was as if he became acutely aware of our fate together. Since my arrival, we had been husband and wife automatically, without feeling. Once, after he had lain with me, his breath did not subside but rose instead in frustration and defeat—defeat at my body's presence when what he wanted most in the world was to be rid of me, and frustration at the two of us together.

As early as London, I suspected that Hsü Chih-mo had a girlfriend. We were on a bus—I think it was the one we took to Southampton for a visit—and I was sitting alone toward the back of the bus, while Hsü Chih-mo and a male friend sat up near the driver in the front of the bus. In the reflection of the driver's big rearview mirror, I could see Hsü Chih-mo and his friend engaged in deep conversation. At one point, and I was not even aware till then that I had been watching them, Hsü Chih-mo motioned his friend to silence, pointing toward me at the rear of the bus. What else would Hsü Chih-mo care to keep from me?

At the same time, I wondered why he would bother to hide it from me. Perhaps he was being very Western about it. In China it was very normal for a man to *na qie*, take a concubine. His family chose the *Da Taitai*, the principal wife, but the man himself picked the *Xiao Taitai*, concubine or concubines, depending on his wealth. The principal wife could not object. In fact it was considered her duty to welcome a concubine into the house. Jealousy was one of the *Qi Chu*, one of the seven reasons a man could divorce a woman.

A man took on a concubine for two reasons. The main one was if the principal wife could not bear a son. Take, for instance, the principal wife of Liang Qichao, Hsü Chih-mo's mentor. She had not borne a son—only a daughter—by her late thirties when she and Liang Qichao were living abroad in Japan. Unable to fulfill her duty to the Liang family, this woman returned to China, chose a concubine, and took this second wife with her back to Japan. She was raised correctly, this principal wife, and knew her responsibilities to the Liang family.

The second reason a man took on a concubine was because he desired her. Lao Ye wanted many women—one each for the north, south, east and west—as the servants used to say. He could have easily invited one of the women to live in the house with us. It would have been Lao Taitai's duty to accept her.

That day on the bus I hated how disappointment rose within me. I tried to keep my eyes fixed on the scenery outside the window. I should have predicted that Hsü Chih-mo had found a girlfriend. Why else had he not sent for me during his past two years in the West?

CHAPTER NINE

BOUND FEET AND
WESTERN DRESS

O nce in college, my boyfriend and I were having breakfast with a young graduate student from China. I don't remember the man's name, only that he was visiting for a day or so, and my boyfriend at the time, David, who was white, studied Chinese and interested in things Chinese (including me), had volunteered through a program to put him up for the night.

It was one of those typical cold New England mornings in Cambridge, and the three of us sat at an early morning breakfast in a nearly empty dining hall. And to my mind, it was one of those typically relaxed breakfasts where I read the newspaper, worried about my upcoming class and for the most part did not interact much with either David or the visiting student. I was meeting him only for that breakfast and, unlike David, did not consider a person from China a novelty.

When I went up to get more coffee, the man remarked to David in Chinese, "*Ta yijing bushi zhongguo ren le.*" She is already not a Chinese anymore.

Afterward, David told this to me and I was livid. What right did this man have to say something like that? How did he know what was Chinese and what was not? Was I less Chinese just because I had been brought up in the West and not in China?

I thought a lot about this man's comment when I read about Hsü Chih-mo's experiences studying in the West. Hsü Chih-mo had left for America in 1918 and graduated from Clark University a year later. He received a master's degree in political science at Columbia University, then began his Ph.D. studies there. In October 1920, he impetuously abandoned these studies and headed over to England. He intended to study with Bertrand Russell but found that Russell was not even in England at the time and, furthermore, had been expelled by his colleagues at Cambridge for his pacifism during the war. Disappointed, Hsü Chih-mo enrolled at the London School of Economics, where he met Goldsworthy Lowes Dickinson, who arranged for him to study at King's College, Cambridge University.

Strolling amid the stately lawns and medieval monuments of Cambridge University in the summer of 1989, I imagined the sensation Hsü Chih-mo must have created here in 1921 and 1922. According to records, the literary critic I. A. Richards invited Hsü Chih-mo to join in the activities of the Heretics' Club, a literary circle devoted to prosody and translation. E. M. Forster later described meeting Hsü Chih-mo as one of the most exciting things that ever happened to him. Dickinson wore continually the Chinese cap that Hsü Chih-mo had given him in admiration.

How exotic, quixotic Hsü Chih-mo must have seemed to his Western friends: an intelligent, extravagantly romantic Chinese discovering kindred spirits and traditions in the West. Hsü Chih-mo had the best of both worlds, I thought. I envied his being able to mix in the Western world so well—better than I, and I was brought up here. How did he do it, become friends with Westerners and not have them call him "Chink," not have them call him names? It seemed that he had everything: the admiration of the Chinese and the admiration of the Westerners.

Or was it that he accepted Englishmen, treated them with a blindness he did not have toward his own fellow countrymen? Toward his own wife? Most of my friends were non-Chinese also. Did that mean that I was like Hsü Chih-mo, a sucker for white faces?

When I was in college I envied those Chinese who associated primarily among themselves, speaking Chinese to one another and hanging around in a large group. They always looked so comfortable. Whereas, whenever I was with other Chinese, I could not help but feel self-conscious, concerned as we walked around campus that others would think we were foreigners, outsiders.

At the same time I could not be with my Western friends and walk by a group of Chinese without wondering what they thought of me. Did they think that I had disdain for my own heritage? I had trouble with everyone. For example, if I walked into a Chinese restaurant and the waiter began speaking in Chinese to me immediately, I felt put upon. But, if he did not speak Chinese with me, I was equally disturbed.

I wanted to go out with Chinese men. However, I also wanted to go out with Western men, but only on the condition that they knew something about China. Yet, Western men who dated mainly Chinese women aroused my suspicion. Did such men consider us Chinese women as more subservient or exotic than our American counterparts? To my even greater distaste were those Westerners who claimed so great an affinity with China that they thought they knew the Chinese better than we knew ourselves. And most of all, I hated anyone, man or woman, who dared attempt explain me to myself!

We moved to a town called Sawston, some six miles from Cambridge University, where, thanks to Goldsworthy Lowes Dickinson, Hsü Chih-mo was going to study as a special student of literature at King's College. We rented a little cottage with two bedrooms and a living room whose bay window overlooked a dirt road. There were only three houses on our street; surrounding us were meadows where sheep grazed. The back of our cottage opened onto a raised porch. Farther away, just like in the back of our family compounds in China, there was a little pond, overgrown with grass and shrubs.

In the beginning, I hoped to learn. Hsü Chih-mo hired a female tutor to come to the house and teach me English. I had gotten through the alphabet and could manage "Good morning" and a little conversation, when the lessons stopped because the woman complained it was too far to walk. Later, I wondered why I did not insist to her or Hsü Chih-mo that we continue the lessons. There were so many other things to do, though: shop, clean and prepare the meals.

Here I had come to England to join my husband and learn Western ways, and all I did was clean house, wash clothes, buy food and cook it. Years later I returned to Sawston with my second husband, Dr. Su, and was amazed at what I had managed to do each day there in the cottage. I had been like a servant back in China, taking the bus to the market and lugging food back to the house. Some weeks, we received packages from the Hsüs—Chinese food and cooking ingredients—but most of the time I was on my own. I do not know how I did it. I did not know anything and the money was always short. Hsü Chih-mo barely gave me enough to cover household expenses. Even the market was a distance: I relied most of the time on a vegetable merchant who stopped his lorry in front of the house and sold me fresh food. How little I knew then! I remember there was this strange machine in the living-room closet. I did not know that it was a vacuum cleaner. So I went on using the broom.

Did I think that my husband would act differently toward me when we were in the West? In China, husband and wife were supposed to act distant toward each other, especially in front of the in-laws, to show respect. But here in the West we were alone, and Hsü Chih-mo and I could have done what we wanted. Only Hsü Chih-mo did, coming and going as if I were not there. Still, he was always home for meals, both dinner and lunch, maybe because we were so poor. If the food was good, he said nothing. If the food was bad, he said nothing. His mind was elsewhere, on books and literature, the East and the West.

You young people today know how to discuss things. You would probably have tried talking things over with your husband, but I felt then that I could not tell Hsü Chih-mo any of my thoughts. I felt I had no language, no words, to say that I knew I was old-fashioned but would change if I could. After all, I was in the West—I could study and try to become learned. But there was no way that Hsü Chih-mo saw who I was. He did not talk to me. I could talk to my brothers, who were just as learned as Hsü Chih-mo, but with my own husband, about anything, it was always, "What do you know? What can you say?" He rode a bicycle to and from the Sawston station to Cambridge or, sometimes, he took the bus to the campus. Each morning, even if he did not go into Cambridge, he rushed out to have his hair cut. This was a habit I did not fully understand. I thought he might just as easily have trimmed his hair at home and saved the money because we always seemed to be waiting for checks from Lao Ye. Still, there were many things Hsü Chih-mo did about which I had no say.

Take Mr. Guo, for instance. His name was Guo Yusheng. I have no idea why this man simply appeared one day and moved in with us. I suppose that Hsü Chih-mo needed the rent money. Then again, if I think about it now, Mr. Guo had probably been living alone and Hsü Chih-mo said how much nicer it would be to live in a house and have someone cook Shanghai food for him. Or maybe Hsü Chih-mo did not want to be alone with me. In any case, Mr. Guo took the other bedroom, which Hsü Chih-mo until then had been using as a study. Unlike Hsü Chih-mo, Mr. Guo did not go into Cambridge very often, studying instead at the cottage all day. So sometimes he would come with me to the market or pick up a few things for me at the local grocery store if he was taking a walk. I was thankful for Mr. Guo's company. At least he would make conversation with me.

I scarcely saw Hsü Chih-mo during the day. He was always at school. Once, though, he took me to Cambridge to see the boat races, and another time to see a Valentino movie. We had to go to the movies during the day because there was no public transportation at night. And we had intended to see a Charlie Chaplin movie, but on the way to that film we ran into a friend of Hsü Chih-mo's who said he thought the Valentino movie was better. Oh, okay, said Hsü Chih-mo, and so we turned around and headed in the opposite direction. Hsü Chih-mo was always like that, happy and good-natured. He was an artist, a dreamer. I am the complete opposite. It bothered me that we had set out to see the Chaplin movie and ended up elsewhere. Hsü Chih-mo and his friend joined the audience in applause when Valentino came on the screen, but I just sat there in the dark with my hands in my lap.

We had a miserable life there in Sawston. Now I read about Cambridge and think about all the lovely things that I might have done. I could have walked along the old bridges and admired the architecture of the buildings. I could have sat on the banks of the river Cam and just enjoyed nature. In Xiashi, I had yearned to get out, walk around and explore. But I had not been allowed on the streets alone. Here in Sawston, I had the opportunity but did not do it.

With the summer heat came signs of life in my body. From A-huan, my child at home, I recognized the nausea and weakness that came upon me in the mornings. In Xiashi, I had wanted to, needed to produce a child. Here, I had no idea what to do. How would I tend house while pregnant? Could I raise a child here? Would I have to return to Xiashi? I deliberated for days how to break the news to Hsü Chih-mo. One afternoon when Mr. Guo was out, I simply told him.

Hsü Chih-mo said instantly, "Get an abortion."

Never in my life had I expected this response. As far as I knew, abortions were dangerous, life-threatening. Only a woman in desperate circumstances—she was having an affair, or the family was starving to death and could not afford to feed another mouth— would risk an abortion.

"I've heard that people die from abortions," I said.

"People die from train accidents," Hsü Chih-mo answered coldly. "Do you see people stop taking the train?" He turned away from me impatiently.

"But where would I get the abortion?" I asked.

He shook his head. "You'll find a place," he said. "It's very common here in the West."

In China the birth of a child, especially a son, is a fortunate event. Children are necessary for the continuity and worship of the family ancestors. Both my parents and my in-laws would have been thrilled. But Hsü Chih-mo was not thinking of these things. He was adopting yet another custom from the West, and wanted me to abort the child, as if its birth were shameful. What would our parents say if they knew he was depriving them of another grandchild?

In the cottage next door to ours lived a Chinese couple, the Hes. They were both studying at Cambridge and had moved to Sawston at Hsü Chih-mo's suggestion. Their cottage was set farther back from the road than ours, and they often cut through our backyard on the way to school. The day after my conversation with Hsü Chih-mo, I was hanging laundry on the back porch, when I saw Mrs. He. I waved to her.

A few minutes later she climbed up the steps to the porch. "You're busy, as usual," she greeted me. "I just thought I'd stop by on my way to town."

I had been thinking all morning about abortions and decided that I would ask Mrs. He what she knew. In case Hsü Chih-mo asked me about it again, I wanted to get information as quickly as I could.

"Well," Mrs. He said casually, leaning on the porch railing as if she and I discussed abortions every day, "they've just established the first birth control clinic in London this year. You can probably get it done over there."

"But would it be safe?" I asked. I fussed at an imaginary spot on the tablecloth I was hanging, and avoided my neighbor's questioning eyes.

"I don't know," she answered. She paused, as if recollecting a fact. "Actually, I have heard that abortions are safer in France than here in England.

"So," she continued emphatically, already concluding the conversation, "if I were you, I would go to France to have it done."

She climbed down the steps of the porch to continue on her way, and I thanked her. Apparently an abortion seemed an easy enough decision for her. How did she know all this information? I wondered. Had she herself had an abortion? Was this what all Chinese women did once they moved to the West?

I did not understand. Our child was a gift from the gods to the Hsü family. Why would anyone want to destroy it? How could Hsü

Chih-mo, the child's father, be so callous? If he was worried about my not being able to raise the child in the West, why didn't I just return to Xiashi to have it?

During our whole married life, Hsü Chih-mo and I had never spoken in depth with each other. But because my brother had picked him for me, and I knew his family upbringing and background, I trusted Hsü Chih-mo. I thought him an honorable man, loyal to his family and clan. I expected to obey him for the rest of my life. Until Hsü Chih-mo told me to get an abortion, doubt about him had never entered my mind.

But now, as the days passed, I found myself questioning this man whose child I carried. Had I been wrong about Hsü Chih-mo all along, merely imagined him as a righteous husband who brought honor to the family with his scholarly genius and who was filial to his parents? If that were the case, then Fourth Brother, Lao Ye and Lao Taitai had been wrong about him too. This I could not believe.

But if Hsü Chih-mo's words were any indication of his thoughts or spirit, he was not the man I had married, the one who wrote dutiful letters home to his parents and obeyed their wishes to treat me like a wife. He was a different man altogether, one Western not just in clothing but in outlook as well. I was bewildered by this change in him. How had it happened? Was it from his friends, Goldie and others that I did not know about, but heard Hsü Chih-mo discuss with Mr. Guo? Was it from his studies and reading? Was this what had changed Hsü Chih-mo?

Second Brother had been in the West for longer than Hsü Chih-mo and had not changed so much in attitude. Perhaps it was not an issue of time but of person; perhaps one was open to it or not. Ever since I was little, I had heard from Second Brother that I had been born into changing times. If so, perhaps now was one of those occasions when I should actively seek change within myself. If I did not want Hsü Chih-mo and me to grow further apart, perhaps that was what I had to do: take a leap of faith and abort the child. I decided I would do so, not to obey Hsü Chih-mo but to understand him. I would make my greatest attempt—even risk my life—for this abortion.

I was still pregnant in early September, when the monthly check from Lao Ye and Lao Taitai arrived, along with a shipment of winter melons and other Chinese vegetables. Abortions were expensive, I was starting to show, and I thought Hsü Chih-mo would now make the arrangements. Although I was prepared to go through with the abortion, Hsü Chih-mo did not bring it up again. I didn't know what this meant. I hoped that he had changed his mind, but as it happened, another matter that had been in the background since my arrival in the West came to the fore.

"We're going to have a guest to the house tonight," Hsü Chih-mo announced to me one morning. "She's a friend from the University of Edinburgh. I'm going to show her around Cambridge and then bring her home to supper with me."

We never had guests to the house, so I was very surprised. But I merely nodded to Hsü Chih-mo and asked what time he wanted dinner.

He said, "Early."

I told him that dinner would be at five.

"Fine," he said, then hurried off to his haircut.

I spent that entire day cleaning, shopping and preparing for dinner. Do you know what I thought? I imagined that I was going to meet Hsü Chih-mo's girlfriend, the woman he would take on as his second wife, his concubine.

From the first moment when I came to the West and saw Hsü Chih-mo talking to his friend in the bus I knew he had a secret.

Later, in Sawston, when he hurried out of the door for a haircut each day after breakfast, and was so intent on telling me about it every morning, I also suspected, although I did not know how, that these early morning departures had to do with the girlfriend.

A few years later I learned from Mr. Guo that Hsü Chih-mo hurried out each morning because he was indeed communicating with his girlfriend, who lived in London. They were using the grocery store down the street from the barbershop as his address away from home. Post was so swift between London and Sawston that Hsü Chih-mo and his girlfriend could pass letters to each other at least daily. They wrote to each other in English just in case I came across the letters, which I never did.

But I knew none of this at the time, only that Hsü Chih-mo was bringing a young woman home for dinner. I only suspected that he had a girlfriend and wondered that he would try to conceal that fact from me. He could have simply announced her to me and had me accept her: that would have been the Chinese way. Even if I had borne him sons, he was entitled to have other women, either to dally with, as did Lao Ye, or to take on as second wives, concubines.

That Hsü Chih-mo wanted us two women to meet signaled to me that she was to be more than just his girlfriend. Most likely she would become his second wife. We would all live under the same roof in this foreign land. Liang Qichao's concubine had joined his family when he was studying in Japan. Apparently Hsü Chih-mo would do the same.

All day long the threat of Hsü Chih-mo's girlfriend appeared before me. She was studying at a university in England; therefore, she was much more learned than I was. She spoke good English, I figured, and was probably as interested in literature as Hsü Chih-mo. Who was her family? Where were they from? Who did they know? Who were her brothers?

At one point during the day I thought maybe Hsü Chih-mo's

girlfriend was a foreign woman. He knew so many of them. Perhaps he was attracted to their open manners, how they threw their heads back when they laughed or wore skirts that revealed their ankles. But I dismissed the idea quickly. No, that could not be. No foreign woman would agree to join a household as a second wife.

I vowed that I would emerge gracious and honorable from this latest indignity thrust upon me by Hsü Chih-mo. I would be firm but accommodating to this new woman, not act jealous or angry. I reassured myself throughout the day that my position in the Hsü family would not change. I had borne a son, I had served his parents. I would always be principal wife.

Strangely enough, I do not recall the name of the woman who came to see us that night; I will just call her Miss Ming. The only thing I really remember about her is how she looked. She was trying very hard to be Western. Her hair was cut short, and she wore dark red lipstick, and a navy woolen jacket and skirt. Looking down past her stockinged legs, I gasped when I saw her feet, two little stumps thrust into embroidered Chinese slippers. So this modern girl had bound feet! I almost laughed aloud.

She was nothing that I had expected her to be. I had thought she would be completely modern. As it turned out later, I was right. Hsü Chih-mo's girlfriend was another woman entirely, one more sophisticated, beautiful, and completely unfettered in her feet. This Miss Ming was not Hsü Chih-mo's girlfriend at all. But I did not know it at the time.

The four of us, including Mr. Guo, sat down to the meal. Miss Ming had been raised outside of Shanghai, too, and she mentioned a few families that I knew, and others that I did not. Her father was in the foreign ministry, but I had not heard of him. I only thought, if her family was so modern as to allow Miss Ming to study abroad alone, why had they bound her feet?

Hsü Chih-mo, Miss Ming and Mr. Guo began discussing English literature, filling their Chinese with words in English so that I could barely follow the conversation. I noticed that Hsü Chih-mo kept looking toward the floor and stealing glances at Miss Ming's feet as he spoke. In spite of myself, I thrust my big feet impatiently under the table, almost kicking Hsü Chih-mo. Why was he treating this girl so much like an equal? She looked so peculiar, the jacket and short skirt completely unbalanced and out of proportion with her tiny feet. What did her parents think about her showing her feet to the world like that?

Hsü Chih-mo confounded me. Was this the woman that he had been seeing since he came to London two years ago? Why her? He always called me a "country bumpkin," and now he was bringing home a woman who, by her feet alone, appeared more backward than I. Yet she was extremely well educated. If Hsü Chih-mo was going to accept a woman like this, why didn't he encourage me to study? Why didn't he allow me to learn English? Why didn't he help me be as modern as a woman with big feet could be?

Why did Hsü Chih-mo want to bring this woman to the household? He did not watch the money carefully, and now we would have another mouth to feed. A thought struck me. Had Hsü Chih-mo wanted me to have an abortion so that we could bring this woman into the house instead of a child? I wanted to cry. What would this woman contribute to the house over our child? Who was she? She was *busan, busi*, neither three nor four. With her bound feet, she would only create more work for me. I would have to do all the shopping and cleaning still, and serve her like Lao Taitai.

After supper Hsü Chih-mo took Miss Ming to the train station.

Mr. Guo retired to his bedroom. I was distracted by the events of the evening and cleared the dishes clumsily, slowly. When Hsü Chih-mo came home I was still in the kitchen washing. He seemed restless and hovered about me. I was so angry, disappointed, and disgusted at him that I could barely speak. After I finished with the dishes, Hsü Chih-mo followed me out to the living room. He asked me what I thought of Miss Ming.

So many thoughts swirled around my head that I said the first thing that came to mind, even though I had vowed to be gracious and accommodating. "Well, she seems fine," I said, because I knew I was supposed to accept his choice of concubine, "but bound feet and Western dress do not go together."

Hsü Chih-mo stopped walking around the room. He whirled on his heel, as if my remark had released all his impatience and frustration. "I *know* that," he suddenly screamed. "That's why I want a divorce."

It was the first time Hsü Chih-mo had ever raised his voice to me. In confusion, astonishment, fear, I fled out the back door. I needed to think; I needed to be alone. The cool evening air rushed into my lungs.

Hsü Chih-mo suddenly appeared next to me on the porch, breathless. "I was worried you were going to commit suicide," he said.

Hsü Chih-mo thought me so old-fashioned, he worried I would hurl myself over the porch railing! I looked out at the darkness of the evening and then back at Hsü Chih-mo, whose anguished face was lit by the light from the living room. For a split second, everything seemed absurdly in place, the pain, the misunderstanding, the chasm between us.

When I went to bed that night, Hsü Chih-mo was still reading in the living room. Very late, though, he crept in, tugging on the sheets as he lowered himself onto the bed. Turning away from me to sleep, his body brushed mine lightly, accidentally, I know, but I felt it as a final contact, the last gesture of our sad intimacy.

For several days we did not speak to each other. This was nothing new, but I now found the silence almost unbearable, filled with the echo of his voice that night. He had never lost his temper like that before, displayed so clearly the extent of his frustration; in that one instant, when he asked me for the divorce, he had destroyed the rhythm of our ways. I could not be sure of him now. When he spoke, I found myself fearing he might raise his voice again. When he did not, I wondered when he might. I scrutinized his face, his movements. He seemed on edge, tense but purposeful each time he walked away from the table and strode out the door. One morning, for the first time, he refused his breakfast completely. From the big window at the front of the cottage, I watched him pedal down the street and wondered what was going to happen next.

Why a divorce? Did he think that I served him or his family poorly? Did he think that I was unwilling to accept a concubine? It made no sense to talk to Hsü Chih-mo about the divorce, I thought. One talked about money and what to eat for dinner. But one did not talk about divorce. If Hsü Chih-mo had asked me for a divorce, that meant it was already too late.

About a week passed, then one day, as suddenly as he had asked for the divorce, Hsü Chih-mo disappeared. When he did not return on a first evening, a second, and even on a third, I thought he might have gone into London to see friends. Mr. Guo, my shopping companion, was still in the cottage, but even he did not know Hsü Chih-mo's whereabouts. It seemed that my husband had simply disappeared, telling no one. All his clothing and toiletries remained. His books lay at the desk, open and untouched since his last sitting; I knew Hsü Chih-mo would have at least remembered his books if he had planned to leave.

But by a week's end he was still nowhere to be seen. Mr. Guo seemed to suspect something was wrong and, early one morning, came down the stairs with his suitcases and said that he too would have to go. Just like that.

My pregnancy, the burden of my body, now terrified me. What was I going to do? Where was Hsü Chih-mo? I could not sleep in the big bed I had once shared with him; I could not move through the rooms of the cottage without feeling I would scream. I was all alone.

It was terrible, those few days in the house. Once I glanced out the back window and saw the neighbors walking across the field. The sight of them startled me; I had not seen another person or talked to anyone in days. But I did not want to go talk to them because I did not think it was any of their business.

Back in Xiashi, when the days grew warm and the first boats appeared on the nearby West Lake, we would change our clothes to light silk and gauze, and a servant would bring out the collection of fans the family used to cool itself with during the summer. On the tray would be folding fans of horn, ivory, pearl and sandalwood, and fans of nine, sixteen, twenty or twenty-four ribs reserved for gentlemen because women never used fans with less than thirty ribs. There would be fans with famous couplets written on them, paintings of birds, trees, beautiful women, everything.

All summer the air would be aflutter with our fans. But then the days would grow cool again, and we would lay the fans aside. So there was a name for me in Chinese to describe how Hsü Chih-mo had left me alone in Sawston. I was an "autumn fan," a deserted wife.

It was at this point, during those days, that I considered taking my own life and that of my child too. It would have been so easy just to disappear and end the sadness. I could have thrown myself over the porch or drowned myself in the pond. I could have closed all the windows in the cottage and turned on the gas. Wasn't that just what Hsü Chih-mo had feared I would do, take my own life? I only stopped myself from thinking such morbid thoughts by remembering the first cardinal rule of filial piety from my *Xiao jing*: "Your body with your hair and your skin is a gift from your parents. You must treasure this gift to be filial." Such teachings seemed to come from a lifetime away.

One morning during this terrible time, I was startled by a knock on the door from a man named Wang Zimei. He said he knew I was alone, and had come from London with a message from Hsü Chih-mo. I invited Mr. Wang in, served tea, and sat across the table from him in tense anticipation.

"Hsü Chih-mo wants to know," Mr. Wang said, pausing and frowning slightly as if searching for my husband's exact words, "—I came to ask you, would you want to be daughter-in-law to the Hsü family but not Hsü Chih-mo's wife?"

I did not answer immediately because it made no sense to me. "What does that mean?" I said finally. "I don't understand."

"If you're willing to do that, then it's all very easy," Mr. Wang continued, as if not hearing me. He took a measured breath. "Hsü Chih-mo doesn't want you."

I tried not to stiffen visibly when he said that, but instead repeated my question. "What does that mean?" I asked. "If Hsü Chih-mo wants a divorce, how can I be the daughter-in-law of the Hsü family?"

Mr. Wang took a sip of tea and looked at me thoughtfully, taking in my hair, face and clothing. He was going to make a report to Hsü Chih-mo, I knew, and the thought angered me. I stuck out my chin at him and remarked suddenly, "Hsü Chih-mo was too busy to come see me on his own? You came all the way out here just to ask me this silly question?"

I saw him to the door, closed it firmly behind him, and knew that Hsü Chih-mo would not return.

Once, long before Hsü Chih-mo had ever mentioned a divorce, Second Brother visited us at the cottage. I had been preparing lunch at the back of the house, just lighting the stove, in fact, when I felt something.

"Someone's coming," I said to Hsü Chih-mo, shutting down the gas and running from the kitchen to the living-room window. It was Second Brother; I knew it was he just by his walk. It took him a full five minutes to come down the road, and I stood by the door the entire time waiting. He had left China shortly after I did and was then living in Paris studying. He had not said he would visit but, with Second Brother, I could just feel things like this. We were that close.

So, it was to Second Brother that I finally turned after Mr. Wang left. I sat at the kitchen table and composed a letter explaining everything. I was three months pregnant, I said, and Hsü Chih-mo wanted me to have an abortion. He said we were like bound feet and Western dress, and wanted to get a divorce. He was nowhere to be found, now, but had just sent a friend over asking if I wanted to be "daughter-in-law to the Hsüs but not his wife." What should I do? I asked Second Brother.

When I finished writing, I went upstairs to the bedroom and reached in the back of my top bureau drawer for a slim pile of letters. These were letters written just to me from Second Brother, separate from the letters Second Brother had written to Hsü Chih-mo and me. Peering at the words written on the back of the envelopes, I returned downstairs and painstakingly copied Second Brother's address. Only because I had studied with that tutor for a short time was I able to copy the letters in English. Still, my writing was crooked and messy, so bad and uneducated. And here I had come to Europe thinking I would learn.

I threw on a sweater and walked to the small grocery store to post the letter. It was growing dark by the time I returned home, and I made myself a simple dinner of rice and cabbage. Then I sat alone in the cottage that night with all the lights out and cried for the first time since Hsü Chih-mo had left.

When the letter came from Second Brother several days later, I tore it open in haste. "Losing Hsü Chih-mo from our family is as sad to me as the death of our parents," Second Brother began, using an old Chinese saying to express grief about the divorce. This was how much Second Brother loved Hsü Chih-mo, as much as his own parents.

"Do not abort the child. I will take it," Second Brother instructed me. "Leave everything behind and come to Paris."

With that, I left Sawston one fall morning, closing the door behind me and carrying as much as I could down the dusty street to the Sawston station. I just quit the house as Hsü Chih-mo himself had. And all I remember by way of regret was leaving behind the winter melons that Lao Ye and Lao Taitai had sent all the way from China.

CHAPTER TEN

A BETTER WIFE

During the five years that I interviewed Yu-i, the only time she ever cried during our interviews was when she described Second Brother's grief following news of the divorce. I could not believe that the Chang family loved Hsü Chih-mo so much.

It pained me to hear how Yu-i had tried to do everything right and had still gotten hurt in the end. Why should she care so much about disappointing her brother and her family with the divorce? She had tried her best to be a good wife to Hsü Chih-mo.

My mother asked me the summer I graduated from college what I wanted to do with my life, and I had no answer. Most of my classmates had taken two-year internships with investment banks, but I returned to my parents' home with no plans and no job. All I wanted to do was continue working on Yu-i's story, to talk with her further, to discuss her life with her.

"And what after the book?" my mother asked.

"I don't know," I said to her. "I can't see beyond it."

"That's all right if you don't know what you want to do," my mother said, obviously still concerned. She waited a beat and then said, "If you just want to get married, that's okay too," and I looked at her in incomprehension because I had not even been thinking along those lines.

At twenty-one, I was the same age as Yu-i when Hsü Chih-mo deserted her in Sawston, and the same age as my mother when she married my father. Although I did expect to share my life with someone in the future, the thought of marriage at the time was out of the question. There was still so much of me that was unformed and unexpressed. I felt unprepared to face the choices or responsibilities of my mother, who had children shortly after marrying and stopped short of receiving her Ph.D. by one year when my father was transferred to New Haven.

When I saw Yu-i after commencement, she of all people asked when I was going to be married.

I answered, "Twenty-eight," just to appease her, as if I had some kind of plan.

"No, no. Too late," Yu-i said. "Twenty-five years old is a good age," she pronounced, as if making a compromise with me.

I did not have a set view of marriage. But I did know that if something like what happened to Yu-i fell upon me, I would be devastated. I was angry and jealous for Yu-i when she told me that Hsü Chih-mo had fallen in love with Lin Huiyin, the beautiful, well-educated seventeen-year-old daughter of Lin Changmin, director of the Chinese Association for the League of Nations. Hsü Chih-mo met Lin Huiyin and her father in London through his mentor, Liang Qichao, in the summer of 1920. Initially, Hsü Chih-mo and Lin Changmin were friends. The two of them used to play literary games, such as trading love letters, with Hsü Chih-mo acting as the older man, and the father acting as the young woman. Eventually Lin Huiyin and Hsü Chih-mo fell in love.

Watching the lives of Yu-i and my mother, I was scared to death of marriage. I didn't want to be a wife; I wanted to be like Lin

Huiyin, both love object and intellectual equal to Hsü Chih-mo. What was it about marriage that turned a woman with a mind of her own into a woman who followed her husband? What was it about being a Chinese wife that you stopped becoming who you might have been? Of course, Yu-i more than survived; my mother completed her doctorate after overseeing the successful education of her three children, all Harvard graduates; and Lin Huiyin married and went on to become a successful architect. Why was it that I felt so beleaguered and confused?

The long walk from the cottage to the Sawston station, the trip across the Channel, the logistics of it all were hazy even after I arrived in Paris and sat with Second Brother in his apartment. My English was so bad then, I had recognized only the word "Paris" as Second Brother had spelled it out for me in his letter. During the entire journey I had searched for that one word distinguishable from all the others.

On the boat crossing the Channel, I made the decision to disobey Hsü Chih-mo for the first time in my life, and to keep my child. During the past year in Sawston, when Hsü Chih-mo treated me coldly, ignored me, even told me to get the abortion, I chose to respect him and obey him as my husband. But when he left me behind in Sawston without settling either the household or the family situation—neglecting his duty to me and to his unborn child—I stopped thinking that he was a good husband. If he was going to desert me in such a fashion, why should I be the good wife and obey his request for an abortion? I would not abandon my child in the same abrupt way Hsü Chih-mo had deserted me in Sawston.

When I arrived in Paris, Second Brother told me that he would adopt the child I bore. At first I thought this the most sensible solution. If there was going to be a divorce, what would I do with the child alone? But during the week I stayed with him I recognized that, no matter how good his intentions, he would not be able to care for my child on his own. Second Brother was still unmarried, and I was the one who took care of the house, while his head was in his philosophy studies. He took French language lessons every day at the University of Paris in order to be able to read the works of French thinkers, and he intended to move to Germany in several months to study at Jena University under Rudolf Euken.

I also thought about Lao Ye and Lao Taitai back in Xiashi. No matter what happened between Hsü Chih-mo and me, I was A-huan's mother. I wanted him to have a brother or sister; I had been blessed with so many. So I thought, if there was a divorce, I would send the child back to China and ask the Hsüs to adopt it.

It made me nervous to talk about going back to China. If there was a divorce, I felt most people would blame me. They would think that I was at fault, because since the old days the man usually divorced the wife. He signed a bill of divorcement that named one or more of the seven recognized grounds for divorce. These traditional reasons were the *Qi Chu*, the "Seven Outs" for a wife:

> *One, if she disobeyed his parents.*
> *Two, if she could not bear him sons.*
> *Three, if she committed adultery.*
> *Four, if she acted jealous and was unwilling to take in a*
> *concubine.*
> *Five, if she were repulsively sick.*
> *Six, if she talked too much.*
> *Seven, if she committed theft.*

If there was a divorce, people might think that I had treated Lao Ye and Lao Taitai poorly, had not accepted Hsü Chih-mo's girlfriend, or maybe even had an affair with Mr. Guo. If they thought I had committed one of the Seven Outs, they would gossip about me, ostracize me.

Second Brother told me not to worry. He said it was clear that I had committed none of these seven wrongs. Also he told me that my thinking was old-fashioned. Now, according to the law as he knew it, divorce was possible if both the man and woman agreed. But, according to the customary rites of filial piety, if the man was under thirty—Hsü Chih-mo was twenty-six—and the woman under twenty-five—I was twenty-one at the time—both families also had to agree.

I wondered what the Hsü family would do when Hsü Chih-mo told them that he wanted to divorce me. Would his parents consent? Lao Ye and Lao Taitai liked me very much and were also old-fashioned. They would probably insist that Hsü Chih-mo stay with me. There was an old saying that said, "If a man likes his wife, but his parents are displeased with her, then he should divorce her. But, if a man does not like his wife and his parents say that she serves us well, then he should behave in all respects to her as a husband." Perhaps Hsü Chih-mo had suggested that I remain "daughter-in-law to the Hsü family, but not the wife of Hsü Chih-mo" because he worried that his parents would not consent.

What about my own parents? I cringed at the thought of telling them and Fourth Brother. They had chosen Hsü Chih-mo especially for me and would grieve so if they learned of his desire to divorce. I had heard that sometimes parents of divorced women, so shamed, refused to take their daughter back into their home. But I had done nothing unchaste or improper. I was sure my parents would welcome me back to the house if I had to live with them. Also I believed that, if my parents had to give their permission for a divorce, they most likely would.

As for myself, I thought, what would be the point of trying to live with Hsü Chih-mo if he did not want to live with me? What could I do but agree?

But how would I support myself as I carried the child to term? I had with me only what Hsü Chih-mo had given me for groceries in Sawston, and some other money I had found around the cottage. I decided that I had to write to the Hsüs and inform them of my condition. I did not tell them that Hsü Chih-mo had asked me for a divorce. I only told them that he and I were living separately: I was staying with Second Brother and studying in France, where the health conditions were thought to be better than in England. I did not mention Hsü Chih-mo at all. I only said that I needed money for my studies and the child.

A few weeks later I received through Second Brother's address a bank check from the Hsüs for two hundred U.S. dollars. Apparently believing my partial story, Lao Ye wrote that he would send me a check every month and that he was happy I was taking care of myself and the baby.

Almost four months pregnant then, I was nauseous nearly every day. Poor Second Brother. He did not know how to care for a woman in my condition. He said that if I was going to carry the child to term I would be safer living with a woman. I agreed. I did not want to leave my brother, but it seemed that if I stayed I would cook and clean for him and therefore tire myself.

A husband and wife Second Brother knew, the Lius, were also studying at the University of Paris. They were living in the countryside to save on rent, but they agreed to let me stay with them for a while for free.

"I told them that you were not feeling well and wanted to stay in one place while Hsü Chih-mo traveled," Second Brother said.

None of us knew where Hsü Chih-mo was at this time, so Second Brother's story seemed plausible. He and I took the hourlong train ride from Paris, then walked another half hour or so from the station to get to the Lius' home. I cannot even remember the name of the village, but it reminded me immediately of Sawston, very small and quiet with low cottages set back from the road. Walking with Second Brother along the dirt road, I hoped I would not be as unhappy here as I had been in Sawston.

Mr. Liu, whose full name was Liu Wendau, had been on the unofficial delegation to the Paris Peace Conference with Liang Qichao and Second Brother. In the 1930s he served as ambassador to Italy. When I met him, he was about thirty, very polite and learned. His wife, Mrs. Liu, was also studying at the university. Both of them looked at me kindly when we were introduced.

Mrs. Liu spoke first. "I hope you will be comfortable staying with us."

"I am so embarrassed imposing upon you like this," I replied.

"No, it's nothing. It's nothing," Mr. Liu interjected. "We respect your brother and Hsü Chih-mo very much and are happy to help out."

Hsü Chih-mo was respected by his friends for his lively mind and spirit; did they know how he treated his family? I smiled and pretended to the Lius that Hsü Chih-mo knew of my whereabouts and was indeed grateful to them for their help.

As Mr. Liu and Second Brother sat down in the living room to talk, Mrs. Liu showed me around the house. Even the house was like the Sawston cottage, only cheerier, with light blue flowered wallpaper instead of yellow, and a mantelpiece of tile instead of brick. My bedroom, which was on the second floor across from theirs, overlooked the street. In one corner of the room stood a washbasin and stand, a small desk and chair. On the other side of the room a single bed and a chaise longue. Next to the window there was a rocking chair whose frilly cushions matched the style of the white curtains.

Mrs. Liu said that she and Mr. Liu spent most of the day away at school but always came home for dinner. She suggested that I begin learning the language and gave me the name of a tutor. What a good idea. I had wanted to study English in Sawston but had not pursued it. French was my second chance. I told Mrs. Liu that I thought it very impressive that both she and Mr. Liu were studying at the university.

Mrs. Liu laughed. "If you only knew what difficulties I had convincing my in-laws to let me come."

She had always wanted to study abroad, she said, and when her husband was given the opportunity to come, she begged her in-laws to send her too. She had already given the family a son, but they were reluctant to let her go. Only after impassioned pleas from both her and Mr. Liu had they convinced his parents to let her go.

Remembering my own battle with my in-laws, I understood Mrs. Liu's predicament exactly. How lucky she had been that Mr. Liu also fought for her to travel to the West; only Second Brother, not Hsü Chih-mo, had championed my cause. A few years later, when I heard that both Mr. Liu and Mrs. Liu had earned their doctorates from the University of Paris, I was so happy.

Mrs. Liu and I returned downstairs to Mr. Liu and Second Brother. We shared a light lunch, and late that afternoon Second Brother headed back to Paris. Although I knew I would be comfortable with the Lius, I felt so sad watching him go.

The Chinese refer to the gradual passage of time over centuries as "the transformation of oceans into mulberry tree orchards," and I believe this type of change came over me the autumn that I spent in the French countryside. When I first moved there, I was uncertain about the divorce. But by the time I left there I had made the decision that I would agree to Hsü Chih-mo's request for a divorce. I would pursue my own legacy, become my own person.

My own growth as a person mirrored the development of the child within me, which I was convinced was a girl. When I got to the French countryside I was four months pregnant. By the time I left, I was nearly eight, and the difference that I felt inside me was tremendous. I knew when the child moved her leg versus her hand; I could feel her fingers brush inside me.

Hsü Chih-mo had compared the two of us to bound feet and Western dress, which initially confused me, because I did not have bound feet. But during the months in the French countryside I realized, in many ways, I had acted as if I did. In Xiashi, I never dared deviate from the in-laws' expectations of me. I never questioned old Chinese customs and traditions.

I had grown up in an educated, forward-looking family who sent their sons abroad to study. Yet I had been bound by the thinking of the past. I would have to find courage in my thoughts and my actions. I was the first woman in my family not to have bound feet, and I had to use this gift to its fullest advantage.

I could go back to China and live with the Hsüs. I could tell them about the divorce and force them to take sides. But that would be running back to China and asking either the Hsüs or my family to take care of me. I remembered my lessons from childhood about zihqi, dignity. I determined to stay in Europe and try to raise my child on my own. Until I could earn my own living I would continue to accept the two hundred dollars a month from the Hsüs in order to care for the daughter that I carried.

The terrible time in Sawston had taught me that I could function on my own; I could not go back to the Hsüs and live in Xiashi like a young girl. No matter what happened, I decided, I would not lean on anyone. I would stand on my own two feet. As a little girl,

I had seen the Chang family lose everything except its name, and move forward from that disgrace. I knew that I had to try to do the same with my own shame.

Watching Mrs. Liu study at night, I remembered myself at the Teachers' College Preparatory School in Suzhou and with the tutor at the Hsüs' home. I, too, had been that determined. I had cherished my learning. If Hsü Chih-mo and I divorced, I decided, I would become a teacher. That way, when I returned to China, I could make my own living and raise my children in the proper fashion.

One evening I was sitting in my room at the top of the house when I heard the sound of a horse and buggy down in the street. I had a visitor. Running to the window, I saw a carriage and, stepping out of it, Seventh Brother! As he paid the driver, I opened the window and called out, "Hey, I'm here. Come on up."

Seventh Brother cried when he saw me, but Seventh Brother always cried. He was the one everyone in the family said was a woman; I had taken most of the male attributes out of Mama, leaving Seventh Brother with only the female attributes. From his soft, high voice to his physical gestures, even his way of thought, Seventh Brother was like a woman. He wanted to know all about what I was eating every day, what I thought of French food, and how I was feeling. He said I did not look well, but he had come from Paris especially to see me, and I could not be cross with him. He himself looked wonderful, even as he dried his tears and said he would never have imagined finding me alone and pregnant, "in such a state," as he said.

He had left China a month earlier and told me that no one at home knew anything about Hsü Chih-mo and me. Not Mama and Baba, nor Lao Taitai and Lao Ye. I had been writing to both families from France, and Lao Ye had been sending me two hundred dollars a month to live, but I never told them the entire truth. Seventh Brother had even met up with Lao Ye and Lao Taitai in Shanghai prior to his departure so Lao Taitai might pass on to Hsü Chih-mo a small package of his favorite candied preserves.

"Where is Hsü Chih-mo?" Seventh Brother asked.

I had not known Hsü Chih-mo's whereabouts since he left me behind in Sawston. I fidgeted with the preserves package and attempted to sound unconcerned. "I don't know. Have you any news?"

But Seventh Brother himself had only heard about me the day before, when he called Second Brother in Germany. Second Brother had left Paris and was now at the University of Jena. Seventh Brother said he himself was going to Germany, not to learn philosophy but to live cheaply; the mark was continuing to fall and it was very affordable there. Although he had reserved a hotel room in Paris, Seventh Brother pulled a chaise longue alongside my bed and spent the night stretched out next to me.

He left the next morning. I was in the kitchen washing the teacups we had used for breakfast when suddenly I knew I had to follow him to Germany. I had to be with someone in the family or I would simply disappear there in the countryside. The Lius were good to me, but they did not take care of me the way I hoped Seventh Brother would. He was like a woman. He could cook, clean and help care for me as I neared the end of my term. I could live with him in Germany and have the child there. According to Mrs. Liu, the hospitals were even safer in Germany than in France.

I called Seventh Brother's hotel in Paris. He had not yet reached it, and I left a message with the desk for him to wait for me there: I would be joining him.

I explained to the Lius that evening that I would be following my brother to Germany. I thanked them for their generosity and packed my few things. I believe I left the Lius almost as quickly as I had left Sawston.

I spent the last month or so of my pregnancy with Seventh Brother in Berlin. On February 24, 1922, I gave birth to my second son. I wished my mother had been there as with A-huan, but I was alone in the hospital room. Seventh Brother did not even come visit me, because he did not think it a man's place in a new mother's room.

I did not say a word during the entire delivery, and afterward the German doctor said to me in French (because I had to speak to him in French) that I was the bravest patient he had ever seen. When he showed me the boy, I almost cried, because I wanted a girl, an image of me, not of Hsü Chih-mo.

I stayed in the hospital for about a week, hemorrhaging badly. When it came time for me to go home to the small apartment Seventh Brother and I shared, I cannot explain what happened. I suddenly felt too scared to take the baby home with me. I did not know the first thing about taking care of an infant in Berlin. Where would I buy the blankets, the bottles, the crib? I had not prepared any of these things beforehand; I guess I thought I could ignore the child until he came. I was overwhelmed with the idea of raising him on my own.

When the doctor made his rounds the next day, I asked him in French, might I be able to leave my son at the hospital for a while?

He frowned and told me that the baby was a very healthy one. There was no need to keep him there.

"Yes, I know," I replied. "But I cannot take care of him." He consulted my charts at the foot of the bed and smiled reassuringly. "You are fine, madame. Don't worry. You are strong enough."

"No, please," I said. "Let me keep him here at the hospital for just a little while. I don't know what I shall do, where I shall go."

I called Seventh Brother from the hospital and he came by to take me home. Throughout my entire term I had not heard from Hsü Chih-mo. But when I returned from the hospital bloated, swollen, weak, and without my son, I finally heard from him. There was an envelope in his handwriting, which looked as though it had been hand-delivered, not mailed.

Seventh Brother said that John Wu had dropped the letter by the apartment. John Wu was a friend of ours who had studied at the University of Michigan Law School and was now in Berlin on another fellowship. Among all the Chinese studying abroad, John was one of the smartest. Later he became president of the Special High Court in Shanghai and translated the Psalms and the New Testament into Chinese.

As Seventh Brother brought my things into my bedroom, I asked him for John Wu's telephone number. John answered, and cleared his throat nervously after I identified myself.

"Yes, well, Hsü Chih-mo asked me to give that letter to you," he explained.

"That means that he's in town," I said. "Where is he? Is he staying with you?" I hated how my voice rose out of control.

"Never mind," John said, sounding upset that he had somehow revealed Chih-mo's whereabouts. "You just read the letter."

Usually Seventh Brother spent the afternoon around the apartment with me, but today he emerged from his bedroom with books in his arms.

"I've got to go study," he called over his shoulder. "I'll be home tonight."

I did not blame Seventh Brother for leaving. Why would he want to get involved with all my troubles? I picked up the letter and held it in my hands for several minutes, considering its contents.

Hsü Chih-mo had waited this long to contact me. I had lived off in the French countryside. I had just delivered his child, not knowing where he was. I had endured so much already on my own. And now this letter. What would it say? Would it tell me that I could be a daughter-in-law to the Hsü family but not Hsü Chih-mo's wife? Would any of it alter the way I felt? Living for half a year separate from him and his family, I knew I could live on my own, no matter how weak I felt at the present moment, no matter what the letter told me.

I slit the envelope open with my finger and unfolded the letter carefully. It was written in Hsü Chih-mo's flowing, very beautiful hand and said that marriage not based on love was intolerable. My husband wanted a divorce from me, and he wrote:

> Real life must be obtained through struggle; real happiness must
> be obtained through struggle; real love must be obtained through
> struggle! Both of us have boundless futures . . . both of us have
> minds set on reforming society; both of us have minds set on
> achieving well-being for mankind. This all hinges on our setting
> ourselves as examples. With courage and resolution, with respect
> to our personalities, we must get a free divorce, thereby
> terminating pain and initiating happiness.

There was no mention of the baby, no mention of his desertion of me in Sawston, no mention of the union that our parents had wished for us. I felt that Hsü Chih-mo was speaking less to me than to a crowd of people, or to historians. What did he mean by our "boundless future" and "our achieving well-being for mankind"? When had I ever displayed any of these potentials? His letter reminded me of that evening in Xiashi when he paced our bedroom and said that he would be the first man in China to get a divorce.

I called John Wu back again and told him that I wanted to speak to Hsü Chih-mo. I figured that Hsü Chih-mo was staying with him. John said that he would not tell me where Hsü Chih-mo was. I said, never mind, that he should just tell Hsü Chih-mo that I would meet him tomorrow morning at his house.

"I want to see Hsü Chih-mo personally," I told John. Because Hsü Chih-mo had asked me for the divorce in a letter! He could not even come to see me personally to ask me about it.

After I talked to John Wu, I ran to the bathroom, because I was still bleeding from the child. I spent the remainder of the day in bed, resting. I wanted to be as strong as possible the following day when I saw Hsü Chih-mo. I had not seen him for six months, and I wanted to show him that I had fared well for myself after he left me behind in Sawston.

When Seventh Brother arrived that evening, he prepared a simple meal for both of us, and we ate quietly. He was too discreet to ask me what had happened, so I did not say anything. I myself still did not know.

The next day I hired a buggy to take me to John Wu's house. He lived far from the center of town in a house with other students, and the carriage made its slow way. John greeted me awkwardly at the door and led me into a large living room with bay windows overlooking a small garden. Around the room were music stands with open books upon them; John apparently studied that way.

Then I saw Hsü Chih-mo. He looked taller and stronger than I had remembered him in our dark cottage in Sawston. I sensed immediately his determination but also his apprehension. Four of his friends were in the house, too, hovering around him as if to embolden him. I knew only two of them, John Wu and Jin Yuelin. Jin had been studying philosophy in the United States and was now visiting here. I spoke first to Hsü Chih-mo because I wanted to show that I was in control.

"If you want a divorce, that's very easy," I began.

"I have already told my parents and they agree," he said.

I could not help the way the tears welled in my eyes at the mention of Lao Ye and Lao Taitai. How had the two of them taken the news?

Then I thought of my own parents. I said to Hsü Chih-mo, "You have parents, I have parents too. If it is possible, let me wait for my parents' permission."

He shook his head impatiently. "No, no, you see, there is no time for that. You have to sign now. Lin Huiyin—" He stopped himself, then continued. "Lin Huiyin is going back to China. I must have the divorce now."

When Hsü Chih-mo mentioned Lin Huiyin's name, I thought, why had he written me all about courage and ideals? He wanted his girlfriend; this was why he was in such a rush. Now, when people ask me if I think that Hsü Chih-mo was revolutionary about the divorce, I answer, no. He had a girlfriend first. If he had divorced me in the very beginning, when he said to me that he wanted to be the first man in China to have a divorce, then I would have believed he was acting on his convictions. Then, I would have said that it took guts for Hsü Chih-mo to divorce me.

All because Hsü Chih-mo was in a rush to get Lin Huiyin, he did not allow me time to get permission from my own parents. I had been raised to be filial, and now I would have to break the union that my parents had willed for me without even asking their permission.

In the silence that accompanied my thoughts, Hsü Chih-mo faced me, seemingly unmoved, his hand clutching the divorce documents.

"Okay, then," I said slowly, steadily, monitoring my breath. My body still ached from the pains of childbirth, and I felt defeated. The only reason I agreed is that I had made the decision in France not to act only on values of the past. I was a modern woman, one of the future. Though it pained me to be so unfilial, I said to Hsü Chih-mo that I would sign the papers without first getting my parents' permission.

"If you think this divorce is the right thing, then I will do it," I said, realizing only afterward that what I said sounded obedient, not modern.

He was very pleased then, smiling as he thrust the papers at me to sign. He could not contain himself. "Wonderful, wonderful. You see, this is so necessary. China must rid itself of the old ways."

He laid the documents on the table and motioned for me to sign. The documents were written in Chinese and said that the two people had decided of their own accord to end their marriage. I was to receive five thousand Chinese yuan as alimony. I never did. Hsü Chih-mo had already signed, and the lines for the four witnesses had already been completed; only my signature was missing.

"There," I said softly, breaking the silence in the room after I signed my name four times. I looked Hsü Chih-mo squarely in the eye as I had been unable to do on our wedding day. "You go get yourself a better wife."

Hsü Chih-mo was so happy. His friends crowded around the two of us with congratulations. They all wanted to shake Hsü Chih-mo's hand. He was jubilant, so very pleased.

He even said thank you to me. He paused dramatically, speaking to me and all his friends and very possibly, I thought, the entire world. "You, Chang Yu-i, didn't want to do it, but you had to. You had to because we had to let others see. We had to have the first divorce."

I nodded, feeling almost nauseous about what I had just done.

These were the same men who would have been at my wedding. How strange they were standing around me at my divorce.

No sooner had I signed the divorce papers than Hsü Chih-mo wanted to go see our child. "Why did you leave him in the hospital?" he wanted to know, and I just thought to myself, What does it matter to you now?

The two of us went to the hospital to stand at the window of the ward and watch the baby in his crib. I felt very odd, as if dissociated from Hsü Chih-mo, our child, even the physical pain that had followed birth. Hsü Chih-mo was entranced, pressing his face eagerly against the glass. He looked at our son with adoration but never once asked me how I was going to feed him, how he was going to live. It seemed that Hsü Chih-mo barely noticed me as the mother of the child. He did not turn toward me once as he marveled at our son. One of the nurses who had cared for me walked by just then, saw me with Hsü Chih-mo, and smiled. So the father was finally able to come, she seemed to be saying, and I wondered if we looked like the other couples in the hospital, young mothers and fathers smiling and happy together as they left with their infants.

CHAPTER ELEVEN

O POET!

The turning point Yu-i experienced in the French countryside reminded me of the so-called "crucial moment" theory my father used to speak of when we were children. Yu-i had pulled herself from despair at a significant time in her life. She could have chosen suicide but instead chose to persevere. I was very proud for her.

Hsü Chih-mo himself had a similar kind of awakening. It was as if the separation from Yu-i, and later the divorce, freed him. In an essay entitled "The Cambridge I Knew," published in 1924, he said that he barely got to know Cambridge when he first settled there was his wife. But in the autumn of 1921 he returned alone for a full academic year.

"Only then did I have the opportunity to approach true Cambridge life, and it was at this time that I gradually discovered Cambridge. Never have I known greater joy," he wrote.

He lolled on the "backs" of Cambridge's colleges admiring the river Cam. He spent hours with friends: Goldsworthy Lowes Dickinson, E. M. Forster, and the literary critic I. A. Richards, even forming an official Anglo-Chinese Society with them.

In one of his earliest surviving poems, a draft dated November 23, 1921, Hsü Chih-mo wrote:

O Poet! How can springtime, that
already has reached out to other men,
Still not release your
Fountains of creative energy?

Laugh, laugh aloud!
The mountain ranges north and south have not yet
spat out all their jewels,
Nor the oceans east and west sprinkled all their pearls.

Soft, soft the sound of pipes, of strings,
Drink deep the light of stars, sun, moon!

O Poet! How can springtime, that already has reached out to
other men,
Still not release your
Fountains of creative energy?

How could Hsü Chih-mo create this airy, spiritual poetry after inflicting all this pain on everyone who loved him? The entire time he was experiencing his epiphany, his pregnant wife had no idea where he was.

Again, I asked Yu-i if she was angry at Hsü Chih-mo, and she always replied, "That's the way it is," or, "That's the way of the artist."

It seemed to me that Yu-i's view of the artist—one who lived outside the responsibilities of reality—was not too far from Hsü Chih-mo's view of himself as poet. He wrote, "The only proper occupation of poets is dreaming. The true poet is one who, deep in dreams, his spirit soaring far above the bright clouds, gives voice at will to random lines and fragments."

Hsü Chih-mo told Yu-i that afternoon in Berlin that he had to secure the divorce immediately because Lin Huiyin was returning to China. Reading about Lin Huiyin, I learned that she and her father were already in China at the time of the divorce; they had left England about five months earlier. So what was Hsü Chih-mo telling Yu-i? Was he lying to her? Or did he intend at the time to return to China immediately to pursue Lin Huiyin? He did not return to China until October 1922, seven months after the divorce. Rather, he returned to Cambridge to continue his final transformation into a poet.

Aware of Lin Huiyin, Yu-i said that she did not think that it took guts for Hsü Chih-mo to divorce her. I was proud of Yu-i. That showed that she really understood what the divorce was supposed to mean.

For my part, I hated the divorce. In writing about Yu-i's life, I had begun to get involved with it to the point that I saw other opportunities and options opening up for her different from what had ultimately happened. Her life had started to take on a fictional reality as I imagined it. Why did she have to divorce? What if Yu-i had been as educated as Lin Huiyin? Would Hsü Chih-mo have fallen in love with Yu-i instead?

According to my own research on divorce, Second Brother had been correct. Most likely Hsü Chih-mo and Yu-i would have divorced under the Draft of the Civil Law, which said that if the husband and wife were not in harmonious terms they could both agree to the divorce. But since Hsü Chih-mo was not yet thirty, and Yu-i not yet twenty-five, the permission of the parents had to be obtained.

Since Yu-i did not get the permission of her parents, was the divorce still legal? I did not find the original documents but felt that the divorce's treatment by the parties involved was more significant than its technical legality. After Yu-i and Hsü Chih-mo signed the papers, the two of them considered themselves divorced. That Yu-i never received five thousand yuan alimony did not bother her. She said with pride that "she never received a penny from the Hsü family for the divorce," when she could have demanded it. Indeed, Yu-i was standing on her own two feet.

I always think of my life as "before Germany" and "after Germany." Before Germany, I was afraid of everything. After Germany, I was afraid of nothing. I stayed in Germany for three years after my divorce and learned a trade of my own as a kindergarten teacher. Other than a few months in Hamburg, I lived in Berlin with my son and a female German companion named Dora Berger. When I returned to China in the spring of 1925, I was a much stronger person who feared nothing.

I owe so much to my time in Germany. Immediately after the divorce and with the baby so young, I felt very nervous about living on my own. I even thought that I would go home to Xiashi and live there with my infant son. But I had promised myself that I would try to stand on my own, and the best place for that type of training was in Europe. Also, I had divorced without my parents' permission, and it would have been very rude of me to return home immediately and flout my disobedience. I had told my parents that Hsü Chih-mo and I were living separately because we wanted to pursue different courses of study. In a few years, I thought, my parents will become accustomed to my living alone in Europe without Hsü Chih-mo. Then I will go home and tell them the truth.

As things turned out, it was very fortunate for me that I spent time on my own in Germany, because when I went back to China people were still talking about the divorce. This was three years later already. Can you imagine? If I had not become my own person in Germany, I would not have been able to bear the attention. I would have felt shameful that I had somehow caused the divorce, not proud that I had survived it. I would have been very upset, not indifferent, that people were talking about me. The worst I ever had to endure was sitting across from two women in a train compartment as they discussed me.

"Chang Yu-i must be very ugly and old-fashioned," one of them said.

The other one agreed. "Why else would Hsü Chih-mo leave her?"

These two women did not know it was me sitting right across from them. Otherwise, they would have been so embarrassed! By that time, after Germany, I knew that what they said was only part of the truth.

I settled in Berlin in 1922. Greater Berlin had just been established two years earlier in a merger involving eight cities, some fifty rural communities and close to thirty farming townships and villages. So, now, Berlin was the largest industrial city on the continent, the major commercial, banking and stock exchange center, the most important railway junction and the second largest inland port of the German Republic. The year I arrived, an eighteen-kilometer highway, the Avus, had just been built, and hotels, cafés, department stores and restaurants were springing up everywhere.

Just four years earlier, Germany had come out of World War I with heavy losses and a shift from an empire to a republic. The fall of the Weimar Republic caused a swift depreciation of the mark. In the morning, one could buy a fur coat; in the evening, with the same amount of money, only a loaf of bread. The mark was very low. Lao Ye sent me the equivalent of two hundred U.S. dollars each month, and I would change the banker's check from China into dollars of small denomination. With just one dollar, it was possible to buy many things. Lao Ye's money let me pay for rent, food, school and the help of the woman who became my closest friend in Germany, Dora Berger.

A kind, soft-spoken woman in her early forties, Dora was a friend of Second Brother's from his first years in Germany, when he studied at the University of Berlin from 1913 to 1915. Dora said that she would be willing to help Second Brother out by living with me and showing me around Berlin in the beginning.

What I would have done without her help, I do not know. She found me a language tutor and helped me apply to the Pestalozzi Furberhaus, a school based on the studies of a Swiss educator. I took intensive German for a few months, then began at the school. By the time I started school I could understand most things. I also chose to study at the level of kindergarten teacher because it required the least amount of language skill.

There were about fifty girls in my section for kindergarten teachers at the Pestalozzi Furberhaus. Because I was going to be with these girls for a long time and did not want to have to think about lying all the time, I told them, if they asked, that I was divorced. They were good about it, never saying anything mean. Most of them had never been married, and when they found out I had an infant son to care for on my own, they were even kinder to me. At *Kaffee*, which we had at four every afternoon, they always came to sit next to me and ask me how things were.

Pestalozzi was a Swiss educational reformer who believed in a completely different kind of education than the one that my brothers had learned under Confucianism. Pestalozzi believed that the individuality of each child was sacred and that children learned by discipline based on love and understanding, not by rote. A Pestalozzi teacher was to encourage a child to absorb knowledge through his own sensory experiences, and to instruct based upon the child's own experiences and observations.

I was very good in the class, my fingers nimbler than most of the other girls in fashioning toys or cutting shapes out of cardboard. One day we were learning to make toy automobiles out of matchboxes, and the teacher was called out of the room. He motioned for me to come to the front of the class, thrust his matchbox into my hands and said, "Here, you teach them to do it while I'm gone."

Each morning, while I attended classes, Dora took care of my baby. She grew to love him as her own, raising him from birth as a German boy so that he spoke only German and ate only German food. I had named him Bide, which sounded like Peter in German, and used the character *de* from *Deguo*, meaning Germany. But we always called him Peter because he was a child of the West. After the daily marketing, Dora took Peter for strolls in the Tiergarten. When I returned in the afternoon after classes, Dora would always tell me about the wonderful things Peter had done that day, that he had smiled for the breadman and sneezed at the monkeys.

She was very good with Peter, always playing with him and telling him how much she loved him. Funny, we Chinese never tell that to our children. We usually scold them and, in paying them this kind of attention, inform them of our love. I liked watching Dora play with Peter; she made all activities a game.

Dora was my first real friend, separate from anyone outside my family. I do not understand why I lost track of her afterward. I tried to write to her but it was so difficult for me to write in German.

We rented three rooms in a big house north of the Tiergarten that belonged to an elderly widow. The salon was reserved for the landlady, and Dora and I lived with Peter in rooms off the hallway. We shared the toilet with the landlady, and a bathtub with its own running water and heater. Our food we kept in our own rooms, but we always cooked in the kitchen and ate, sometimes with the landlady, in the common dining room.

It was good that Dora lived with me because I think that a Chinese woman alone with her child looking for rooms might have been refused on her own. As it was, we moved quite a few times because Dora was very particular. If something was not clean, or if the landlady complained about children or Chinese people in her house, Dora would not stand for it, and we would leave.

We lived in maybe three or four different apartments in Berlin and tried different stories on each of the landladies: that Peter's father was dead, that he was finishing his studies in England while I pursued my work in Germany. We even told one landlady the truth, that I was divorced, but she looked at me with such suspicion, as if I were a criminal, that I felt uncomfortable. In the beginning I could not speak German well, so I suffered everyone talking around me to Dora. They were always worried we could not pay, and then we would have to say that my rich family was supporting both of us, or that I was on a generous stipend from the Chinese government, and money was no problem. Still, as long as we paid in advance and on the first of the month, the landladies did not complain.

Dora herself came from Vienna and had never been married, even though she was over forty. I saw many women like that in Germany. I never asked Dora much about her past because I thought it was none of my business. But once she told me her story: that she had waited for a childhood sweetheart who left her behind in their hometown when he set out to pursue a trade. Then he had married another and not told Dora for many years until she was too old to marry.

Peter was a beautiful child with very large eyes and soft black hair. When we went out walking with him, people would always approach us. He loved music most of all, any kind except Chinese opera, which made him cover his ears with his hands when I played it on our phonograph. But Dora would put on Wagner and Beethoven, and he was content, even attempting to conduct the pieces with a real conductor's baton I bought for him. When he was fussy, I'd turn on the phonograph, and Peter would instantly stop and listen intently. And, if Dora was late coming home from a walk with the little boy, I knew they had probably paused too long by the building of the neighborhood pianist who practiced with his windows open.

I spent all of my time with Dora and Peter. I felt that the other Chinese in the city were all too scholarly for me. Once or twice I tried joining these people at the opera or sailing on the Wannsee. But I was not part of their group. I did not know enough to talk about politics and literature. And, sometimes, I think that the only reason they called me was because of the divorce.

"Oh, you are Chang Yu-i," one once said when we were introduced. If I had been Hsü Chih-mo's wife, he would have ignored me completely because I was not as learned as Hsü Chih-mo. Only now, because of the divorce, I was modern too.

I was different from these Chinese. They could act wild in the West but return to their families and live as they had in the past. Now that I was divorced, I was not sure where or how I was going to live when I returned to China. Lao Ye supported me financially in Germany because I cared for a Hsü son. But what about when I returned to China? Would I have to give Peter over to the Hsü family and live on my own? If I wanted to live with my sons, would the elder Hsüs consider me Hsü Chih-mo's wife even though Hsü Chih-mo and I were divorced?

Of all the Chinese, there was one who was particularly kind to me. His name was Lu Jiaren, and he visited me several times a week. He had very big hands that were hairy like a bear's, and he would sit with me and play with Peter. I had never sat close with a man like this before, but figured that he came to see Peter. Whenever Lu Jiaren visited, Peter stayed in the sitting room with me. With other guests, I sent Peter out with Dora.

Lu Jiaren asked me one day as we were sitting with tea and Peter was playing on a blanket spread on the floor, "Do you plan to marry again?"

I was still very young then, only about twenty-three, but Fourth Brother had written me that I was not to be seen with a man for the next five years to uphold our family honor. Otherwise, people would think that Hsü Chih-mo divorced me because I had been unchaste.

Also, I knew that I had a son at home whom I had not yet educated; I could not marry into another household until I properly fulfilled my duties as a mother.

So I dared not acknowledge the tender tone in Lu Jiaren's voice, and instead, looking into my teacup, said softly, "No, I do not."

Lu Jiaren left shortly afterward and did not visit me regularly after that afternoon. I felt very uncomfortable that he had asked me about marriage; I had never said anything to encourage him. But perhaps I should not have allowed him to make all those visits. Had he been courting me? Was that how "free choice" worked? Was he in love with me? I could not believe that anyone would fall in love with me. So maybe he was trying to marry me to be honorable?

During this time I corresponded regularly with Lao Ye and Lao Taitai and in this manner heard about Hsü Chih-mo. In April 1923, Hsü Chih-mo and Second Brother invited Rabindranath Tagore—the Nobel Prize laureate Bengali poet, Hindu mystic and teacher—to China. Hsü Chih-mo and Lin Huiyin accompanied him on his two-week tour through China, acting as his interpreters. All the Chinese papers carried pictures of them. One reporter compared the three of them to the three friends of winter: Lin Huiyin, the plum blossom; Hsü Chih-mo, the bamboo; and Tagore, with his long white beard and robe, the pine tree.

It was strange to hear such news from China and to know that I could be there too.

"Come home," Lao Taitai would write me as if nothing had happened. "Why don't you come home?"

My husband did not want me, but my in-laws did. "I can't come," I would tell them. "I'm divorced."

"But you're still our daughter-in-law. You'll be our adopted daughter," Lao Taitai always wrote back.

It now made sense to me why Hsü Chih-mo suggested that I be daughter-in-law to the Hsü family but not the wife of Hsü Chih-mo. As far as Lao Ye and Lao Taitai were concerned, I was still the woman they had chosen for their son. I had served them well, given them two male descendants; I had done everything I was supposed to do. Hsü Chih-mo's outright disobedience of their arrangement left them shocked, angered, embarrassed and wounded. But I could not explain to them what Hsü Chih-mo had wanted. Nor could I explain to my in-laws that I was not abandoning them.

"I can't come home," I would finally reply. "I'd feel uncomfortable."

Shortly after his first year, Peter began to have sick spells, very bad diarrhea and at the same time breathing difficulties. Dora and I took him to a doctor that someone recommended. His name was Dr. Hess. At first he could find nothing wrong with Peter. But in the spring of 1923, when Peter was a year and a half old, Dr. Hess and his colleagues discovered a worm in his small intestine. They said that Peter had contracted the worm from bad milk. It was located directly between the intestine and his skin, and there was no way to get at it. Dr. Hess suggested a clinic in Switzerland, but he told me that it was very expensive and that there was no guarantee.

The Chinese believe that the intestines are the storehouse for compassion and affection. It was very sad that so loving a child as Peter should be affected there. Maybe because I did not breast-feed Peter on my own, he got sick. I cannot be sure. I wrote to Lao Ye and Lao Taitai informing them of the diagnosis and asked them to help me make a decision. Lao Ye and Lao Taitai wrote back saying that there was nothing to be done; there was not enough money to send Peter to Switzerland. My in-laws were very wealthy, so I never understood this. Maybe Lao Ye was losing money with the warlord situation in China, I do not know. If they had only met Peter, maybe things would have been different. But he was my child, a child of the West, and would never live to see China.

By the winter of 1924, Peter could not rest day or night and it horrified me to see my child in such pain. He breathed only with great effort. To comfort him, we played the phonograph until the same songs echoed in my ears and the neighbors complained of the noise at night. First he could eat no meat, then no bread, then not even soup. Still, his belly grew bigger, swollen, and the other parts of his body, thinner as the days passed.

One night, after a long bad spell, I woke to hear him yelling loudly. I thought he was having a nightmare and, rushing to his bedside, discovered him wide awake. He was clenching his stomach and calling to me in German, "Mommy, Peter hurts."

We rushed him to the Children's Hospital and Dr. Hess, who had originally diagnosed the illness, took Peter under his charge. He died on March 19, 1925, a little less than a month after his third birthday. Dora and I had known for over half his life that he would die, but when it finally happened, we were both in shock. We could barely cry, move or eat.

We had him cremated and held a ceremony for him afterward. About thirty people attended: Lu Jiaren, some of Second Brother's friends, some of the girls from school and even a woman Dora and I saw regularly in the park. How they had all heard about it I did not know.

Dora and I left the urn at the funeral home. After I moved to Hamburg for the next level of the Pestalozzi Furberhaus, I returned to Berlin to pick up the urn and take it home with me to Xiashi.

The night after the funeral, I woke in the dark to hear Dora in the other room crying, her wails muffled in the pillow. I realized then that she had loved Peter as much as I did. We three had been a family.

With Peter gone, Dora returned to her parents' home in Vienna. After she and I separated, I never spoke to her again or even wrote to her. Although I spoke German fluently, I could not write well enough to express what I felt. I did receive one letter from her, however. It was a brief note with a photograph of her desk at home. At first I thought it strange she would send me such a photograph. But then I saw displayed in the most prominent spot amid all her mementos a large photograph of Peter. This was how much Dora had loved him.

A few years later, when I was already back in China, I learned the sad news of Dora's own death. Apparently physically and emotionally broken after Peter, she contracted pneumonia and never recovered. My little family in Germany had lasted only a brief time.

Hsü Chih-mo arrived in Berlin on March 26, 1925, exactly one week after Peter's death. I had not seen him since our divorce, already three years ago, and he glowed while I stood small and frail in the wake of Peter's death. So many wonderful things had happened to Hsü Chih-mo since our divorce. He had returned to China in October 1922 and published a collection of poems, acted as interpreter for Tagore and, most recently, edited the prestigious *Chenbao* literary supplement.

I was surprised to see Hsü Chih-mo, of course. He said that Lao Taitai had been extremely worried about me with Peter's death and urged him to come. I took him to the funeral home. Clutching the urn of Peter's ashes, he wept. According to the Chinese way, I had ordered the body cremated within three days of the death, but if I had known Hsü Chih-mo would arrive so soon afterward, I might have waited for him to view the body.

CHAPTER TWELVE

SENTIMENTAL JOURNEY

S everal months after the divorce, Hsü Chih-mo returned to China and published his first volume of poetry, *Poems of Chih-mo*. The verse was an immediate success. He was hailed as the most promising poet of 1925 and became responsible for introducing Western rhymes, meters and themes in his essays and poems.

His treatment of Yu-i had attracted the attention of his mentor, Liang Qichao. In a long letter to Hsü Chih-mo in January 1923, Liang Qichao wrote:

> *Hitherto, because I thought there had truly been basic*
> *incompatibilities between you and your wife (even if you don't*
> *want to call her that, I shall continue to do so), I hadn't wanted*
> *to pursue the matter further. But now I gather that since your*
> *return to China you have gone on writing to her and continue to*
> *sing her praises. Why then did you act as you did? It's really*
> *incomprehensible.*

I felt somewhat vindicated reading Liang Qichao's letter to Hsü Chih-mo as he scolded him for causing pain to Yu-i, his two sons, the elder Hsüs and Changs.

"It is the possibility of responding to other people emotionally that places humans above the other creatures, and we cannot seek to gain our own happiness if that is at the expense of someone else's sufferings," Liang Qichao wrote.

Lin Huiyin was promised to Liang Qichao's son, Liang Sicheng. Liang Qichao loved Hsü Chih-mo almost as a son, and yet Hsü Chih-mo wanted to marry the woman Liang Qichao had already chosen for his own son.

Reading Hsü Chih-mo's reply to Liang Qichao, I disagreed with Yu-i and believed that Hsü Chih-mo had divorced for ideals and not merely for Lin Huiyin:

> *I brave the adverse criticisms of society and struggle with all my energy, not so as to avoid the pains of a miserable lot but to seek the calm of my conscience, the first establishment of my personality, and the salvation of my soul.*
>
> *Among men, who does not seek virtuous mediocrity? Who does not feel content with the status quo? Who does not fear difficulty and danger? Yet there are those who break loose and go beyond. I shall search for my soul's companion amidst the sea of humanity; if I find her, that is my fortune. If not, let that be my fate.*
>
> *Alas, my teacher! I have striven in the inner recesses of my soul to create a pure jewel out of my ideals; I nourish it with the hot blood that fills my heart, so that it will shine forth my deepest yearnings.*

I spoke with a woman who knew Lin Huiyin personally, Wilma Fairbank, the wife of a Harvard professor of Chinese studies, John

Fairbank. Mrs. Fairbank said that she thought Hsü Chih-mo's and Lin Huiyin's relationship was romantic rather than sexual, more a literary relationship. She said that whenever Lin Huiyin talked about Hsü Chih-mo she mentioned Shelley and Byron, other poets. She thought that Lin Huiyin always associated Hsü Chih-mo with this type of romantic love.

Lin Huiyin loved Hsü Chih-mo, Mrs. Fairbank said, but she could not marry him. Lin Huiyin herself was the only child of the first concubine. The father favored the second concubine, who had borne him a son. Mrs. Fairbank said that Lin Huiyin could not imagine being in a relationship in which a woman had been cast aside for her.

I told Yu-i these aspects of Lin Huiyin's background, but Yu-i still blamed the young woman for the divorce. She said that if Hsü Chih-mo could not make a decision about a movie, how could he make one about a divorce? He must have had encouragement.

I read to Yu-i from the memorial essay Hsü Chih-mo wrote for Peter called "Wode Bide," My Peter.

> *Peter, my dear Peter . . . You shall never be able to hear these words, yet through mourning you, I wanted to somehow give vent to my suppressed emotions. In this unnatural world, there are many other people in my similar, or even worse, condition and experience. Perhaps these are people who will listen to what I want to say, and will have sympathy for me. Say, for example, your mother, Peter; did she ever have a single day of happiness and joy? Nevertheless, in her equally miserable condition, she showed wisdom, patience, and more impressively, courage and determination. At least she, I daresay, will fully understand the nuances of my words. And I daresay, only she,*

given the chance, is the most qualified to interpret the truth of my feelings. . . .

Peter, I said I wanted to take this opportunity to give expression to my suppressed emotions over the years. But this is by no means easy. What I want to say seems on the tip of my tongue, but when I try to articulate it, it becomes unspeakable. My words are like young tender grass growing under a heavy rock. I need strength to lift this heavy rock and pull the tender grass from its roots without damaging it. God knows how deep the roots have grown! Are they roots of hatred, grievance, remorse, or melancholy? Perhaps they are roots of hatred, grievance, remorse, and melancholy.

Only when a wayfarer's shinbones and ankles get stung by thorns does he realize how difficult this road is. But why are there thorns in the first place? Do they grow there by themselves, or are they planted there deliberately by someone else? Or perhaps they are planted there by the wayfarer himself? Anyway, you cannot put all the blame on these thorns, because this is the road you chose to walk, and the wound is the result of stepping on the thorns; the thorns do not come to sting you of their own accord. . . .

Peter, you came to this mortal world as if a guest, only for a short stay. What you knew was the love from your kind mother, the warmth of the sunshine, the prettiness of the flowers and the grass. When you left your mother's bosom, you returned to the embrace of God. And I am sure he is now listening joyfully to the report of your stay on this earth. . . . Your little feet were never touched by those merciless thorns, and the white clothes you wore when you came were never stained by the mud.

Reading the memorial, I could not help but be struck by the complexity of Hsü Chih-mo's character. Why was Peter's death so close to Hsü Chih-mo? Was it merely his trying to sound like a good father, or was it more? Did he feel guilty that he had initially told Yu-i to abort the child? It sounded to me as if he somehow regretted the divorce. So, perhaps, he had begun to appreciate Yu-i.

I could not believe, however, that Hsü Chih-mo had seen his child only once, yet dared write a memorial to him.

"Well," Yu-i said after she had carefully listened to the essay. "This sounds like a man who cares very much about family and takes responsibilities.

"But," she continued, "judging from his actions, I do not think he worried about these things—whether we had enough money or how we lived. You see, that is the way it is with the artist."

Hsü Chih-mo and I went to Italy together after Peter's death. He asked me to go, and I felt that I needed to get away for a little rest. I had not taken a holiday for four years, since I left China. In China, I would have observed forty-nine days of mourning, but here in Europe it seemed more appropriate for me to travel and try to forget.

Was it strange for Hsü Chih-mo and me to travel together? Well, I did not intend to share a hotel room or sit around in the lobby waiting for him. Not like in London when we were married. As it was, Hsü Chih-mo and I also ended up going with two British women who were friends of his, the Taylor sisters. The sisters and I communicated with each other in basic French—I still did not speak English—and I usually spent the day with them, while Hsü Chih-mo wandered around the sights on his own.

At breakfast every morning Hsü Chih-mo waited anxiously for a letter or telegram from his friend Hu Shi in China. This early morning impatience reminded me of his behavior in Sawston. A few months later I learned that I was not far from wrong. Hsü Chih-mo had fallen in love again, this time with a Beijing socialite named Lu Xiaoman. The only problem was, she was married. Her husband, chief of police in Manchuria, had discovered the affair and threatened to kill Hsü Chih-mo.

Each morning at breakfast Hsü Chih-mo was receiving letters telling him when it would be safe to return to China.

Finally, one morning, Hsü Chih-mo looked up from a letter and said: "Good, we can leave now." Hu Shi had sent word that it was safe to go home. The husband had changed his mind and decided to grant Lu Xiaoman a divorce instead of trying to kill Hsü Chih-mo.

Over the years I have pieced together all the information. Hsü Chih-mo met Lu Xiaoman in the summer of 1924 in Beijing. She was a beautiful twenty-year-old, the favorite at diplomatic events. If she did not attend a party, for instance, people were disappointed. The daughter of a leading minister, Lu Xiaoman spoke French and English; she could paint, write, dance and sing. In 1920 a marriage had been arranged for her with Wang Geng, a handsome Princeton and West Point graduate who spoke English, French and German fluently.

The young couple first lived in Beijing and met Hsü Chih-mo through acquaintances. When Wang Geng accepted a post as chief of police in Manchuria, Lu Xiaoman did not want to leave Beijing, so Wang Geng left her behind with her parents. He asked Hsü Chih-mo to accompany Lu Xiaoman to various functions. People said that the friendship between Hsü Chih-mo and Lu Xiaoman blossomed at this point. Other people said that Hsü Chih-mo met Lu Xiaoman when the two of them acted on stage together for a charity performance. He played the hero, an old scholar, and she was the heroine, a cute maid. After the play the two of them supposedly fell in love.

When Hsü Chih-mo was in Italy with me, he was supposedly on a "sentimental journey" to test the love between him and Lu Xiaoman. He stayed away for five months, not returning to China until August. By this time I had moved from Berlin and settled in Hamburg for the next level of school.

I did not get to know Hamburg as I had Berlin. Dora was gone, Peter was gone, even Second Brother had left Jena and returned to China. I did not have my family in Germany anymore, and sometimes, it seemed, the family in China was so distracted by Hsü Chih-mo and Lu Xiaoman, they forgot about me. The monthly check from Lao Ye and Lao Taitai began to arrive late, irregularly. I needed money for rent, food and ferry transport to school each day. Once, the check was so late, I divided my remaining money and food, a sack of potatoes, into ten piles each.

The check will come in ten days, I told myself. Luckily, it did.

But I was extremely depressed after Peter's death. I began to feel that it did not matter whether I completed my studies at the Pestalozzi Furberhaus. Peter was gone—I could not teach him—and I had already missed A-huan's developmental years. As it was, with what I already knew, I felt certain that I could get a job teaching and support myself in China.

In the spring, letters started arriving from Hsü Chih-mo and the elder Hsüs. Wang Geng's and Lu Xiaoman's divorce had gone through. But Lu Xiaoman's mother would not let Lu Xiaoman marry Hsü Chih-mo until she knew for certain that he was divorced from me: she did not want Lu Xiaoman to take concubine status. Also, Lao Ye and Lao Taitai would not let Hsü Chih-mo marry Lu Xiaoman until I gave my approval in person. The Hsüs and Hsü Chih-mo wanted me to return to China immediately. I was one of the parties involved.

Returning to China at the request of Lao Ye and Lao Taitai gave me face and showed that they still respected me. I returned to China to help them. I could not let the elder Hsüs think that I did not care what happened to the reputation of the Hsü family as Hsü Chih-mo went around with Lu Xiaoman. I wanted to give my approval and set things right. Also, my going home during the height of the scandal between Hsü Chih-mo and Lu Xiaoman would make it clear to everyone that I had willingly agreed to the divorce, and that I had survived on my own since then.

My brothers have always had the knack of showing up in my life at opportune moments. This time Eighth Brother, your grandfather, showed up at the door to escort me back home. Of all my brothers, your grandfather reminded me most of Hsü Chih-mo. When he came to see me in Hamburg, he had just spent the past five years studying at Clark and Columbia universities, the same schools where Hsü Chih-mo had studied. Now he suggested that we travel together to China in the same fashion that Hsü Chih-mo had come to Europe before, by the Trans-Siberian Railway. I have always thought it a pity you never met Hsü Chih-mo, but I am happy that you got to know your grandfather. Although six years apart in age, the two of them were very similar: dreamers with generous spirits.

During my five years in Europe, Mama and Baba had moved from the family home in Nanchang to a house in Shanghai proper, sent most of my brothers abroad for study, and married off all but one of my sisters, Fourth Sister. Greeting them at the train station, I felt I had been away a lifetime. The two of them had aged considerably during my absence.

"Don't cry," I comforted Mama as she hugged me and wept uncontrollably on my shoulder. Neither I nor any of my siblings had ever told her directly about the divorce, but I was sure that she had come to her own conclusions about Hsü Chih-mo and me. "If I'm happy on my own," I told her, still not mentioning the divorce, "that's what is most important."

After we returned home, Baba asked me all about my life in Germany. This was his way of telling me, without bringing up my divorce, that I had fared well for myself. I was thrilled that he did not scold or renounce me for parting with the traditional ways. I had always thought my father old-fashioned. But apparently, even he could not ignore what was taking place in our country. Western ways had come to China. Just during the rickshaw ride from the train station to the house I saw such changes for myself: men with hair slicked back and pointed leather shoes, girls with waved and bobbed hair, in white gauze shirts with tight brassieres clearly visible underneath, knee-length skirts and high-heeled shoes worn over flesh-colored silk stockings.

I went from my parents' home to meet Lao Ye and Lao Taitai at their Shanghai hotel suite. Walking into the sitting room, I greeted each of them with a low bow and nodded briefly at Hsü Chih-mo, who sat on a sofa at the far end of the room. I noticed a large ring on his finger of the purest green I had ever seen. This type of green was called "stop horse jade." A prince once saved his life by directing his jade ring at a charging horse. When the horse saw the vibrant green, he thought it was grass and dropped his head instantly to graze.

"Is it true," Lao Ye said slowly, breaking a strained silence, "that you and my son have divorced?"

Of course, Lao Ye and Lao Taitai knew, but no matter what a piece of paper said, or what Hsü Chih-mo told them, they wanted to hear it from me.

"Yes," I said in as even and neutral a tone as possible.

Hsü Chih-mo made a sound like a grunt and leaned forward in his chair. Lao Ye looked confused and almost sad at my reply.

"Do you have any objections to his marrying Lu Xiaoman?" Lao Ye asked me. He used the word for marriage instead of "taking on a concubine," I noticed. He had obviously believed me about the divorce.

"No," I said, shaking my head. Lao Ye turned away, as if he were disappointed in me. Judging from his reactions, I suspected he had held me out as the last glimmer of hope in convincing Hsü Chih-mo to mend his ways.

Hsü Chih-mo screamed, leaping from his chair in joy. He flung his arms out in delight, as if to embrace the world, and his jade ring flew out the open window. Hsü Chih-mo's expression quickly changed to horror. The ring was Lu Xiaoman's engagement gift to him.

We all looked in the yard below, but he did not find it. How very strange that he should lose it just as I, in effect, gave permission for him to marry. It would be an omen of things to come with Lu Xiaoman.

A few months later, Hsü Chih-mo actually invited me to attend his wedding to Lu Xiaoman. Of course, I did not go; even his parents stayed home. But I know that on his wedding day, Hsü Chih-mo recognized that I had cleared the way for him to marry Lu Xiaoman.

My original intention upon returning to China was to live in Xiashi near the Hsüs. I wanted to live in a little home of my own and open a school for young girls in the area. I even located a building that would have been perfect for my school. But, after staying with my in-laws for a few weeks, I took my son and moved to Beijing.

A-huan had been three, just about Peter's age, when I left him behind in China. Five years later, he had grown into a little gentleman with a striking resemblance to Hsü Chih-mo, that same fairness of skin and delicate bone structure. So very different from my robust Peter, the brother I had always wanted him to meet. Educated at home by a private tutor since the age of four, A-huan appeared to be doing well in his studies. I listened to him read and admired his obvious enjoyment in poetry. I worried, though, about the other aspects of his development. I wanted my son to learn at an early age to be self-sufficient. But that was not how the Hsüs, who had been his guardians for the past several years, had raised him. He did not dress without the help of servants, and he ate candy the whole day long. One afternoon, when no one else was around, I opened his mouth to look at his teeth and saw that most of them had rotted away. This explained why he always asked the cook for soft mushy meats like *shizitou*, "Lion's Head" meatballs, and *huiguorou*, double-cooked pork.

As for myself, I found that I could not live in Xiashi again. I could not be comfortable in a village where people still thought of me as the Hsü wife even though I was divorced. Mainly though, I could not raise my son the way I wanted to in my in-laws' house. I appealed to their abiding concern for their grandson's safety and explained that it was better for A-huan to live in the city. China was in the hands of various provincial warlords, and skirmishes often broke out in the countryside at that time. Also, A-huan could continue his education at a higher level in Beijing. To my surprise, Lao Ye and Lao Taitai agreed. I appreciated their trust in me even after Peter's death. As I made arrangements to move to Beijing with A-huan, Lao Ye informed me that he would divide his income evenly, one third to Hsü Chih-mo and Lu Xiaoman, one third to me and my son, and one third for him and Lao Taitai. I was to receive three hundred dollars a month, which would allow me to raise my son on my own terms.

About one month after Hsü Chih-mo's and Lu Xiaoman's wedding, I received a telegram from Lao Ye and Lao Taitai from a town north of Beijing called Tianjin. I was surprised that the elder couple were so close by; I had thought them in Xiashi.

The telegram said: PLEASE BRING ONE SERVANT AND MEET US AT OUR HOTEL.

When I arrived at Tianjin, I had never seen Lao Ye and Lao Taitai looking so distraught. Apparently Hsü Chih-mo and Lu Xiaoman had gone to Xiashi for a visit after their wedding.

"Lu Xiaoman was just coming to visit us," Lao Taitai began, bristling at the memory, "but she demanded the red bridal sedan chair!" This chair required six bearers, instead of the normal two, and was the chair a woman used just once in her lifetime.

"Then," Lao Taitai continued, her words coming so fast they tumbled over one another, "at dinner, she ate only half her bowl of rice. 'Chih-mo, finish this for me,' she whined."

This, I thought, was etiquette that even eight-year-old A-huan knew. Rice was the food of the country, to be respected in all its phases: the ripe grain in the husk, the paddy, glutinous rice, rice in the straw, hulled rice and cooked rice. To honor the farmers who planted, tilled, harvested and husked the rice, one was not supposed to leave even one kernel at the bottom of one's ricebowl.

"The rice was cold, too," Lao Taitai said, "Hsü Chih-mo might have gotten sick.

"Now, listen to what Lu Xiaoman did next," Lao Taitai said. "After the meal, as we were about to make our way upstairs, Lu Xiaoman turned to Hsü Chih-mo and whined, 'Chih-mo, carry me up the stairs.' "

I had always thought peculiar this particular Western custom, carrying the woman over the threshold. And the stairs at the Xiashi house were extremely long, about fifty steps.

"Did you ever hear of such laziness?" Lao Taitai fairly shrieked to me. "This is a grown woman. She wants my son to carry her. And she doesn't even have bound feet!

"That night, Lao Ye said to me, 'I am going to take the next train out of here. You prepare the bags, and talk to the servants, and join me when you can.'

"So we've come north to be with you," Lao Taitai finished. "You're our daughter-in-law."

What an uncomfortable position Lao Ye and Lao Taitai put me in! I knew that Hsü Chih-mo would be upset. Sure enough, when I took my in-laws from Tianjin to my home in Beijing, I got a call from Hsü Chih-mo.

"You wrote them and told them to come, didn't you?" he asked me.

"No," I replied. "Why would I do that?"

"This has made Lu Xiaoman lose face," Hsü Chih-mo said.

I had not told the Hsüs to come. It was just that the older couple did not understand Lu Xiaoman's new ways. The Hsüs moved in with me shortly before the three-month celebration for the lunar new year. We passed the holidays together, and it seemed like old times again. There were numerous gifts for A-huan, and Lao Ye and Lao Taitai even remembered my birthday on the twenty-ninth day of the last lunar month. I tried not to worry about Hsü Chih-mo and Lu Xiaoman out in Xiashi alone.

As it turned out, the Hsüs returned to Xiashi shortly after the new year because I received a telegram telling me that Mama was very sick. I immediately left for Shanghai, taking the Hsüs with me. They stayed in a hotel at first, then returned to Xiashi, where Hsü Chih-mo and Lu Xiaoman were still staying.

My mother died within ten days after my arrival. She was sixty-three years old. All my brothers and sisters gathered around Mama's bed to mourn her loss. I made all the funeral arrangements.

Just before Mama died, as she drew her last breath, I placed in her mouth a cloth pack containing a pearl, a ruby and a piece of jade, gold and silver. This was food for the dragon who would allow Mama entrance into the underworld.

Then I told the servants to wash Mama's body and dress her in seven layers of seven different colors. The first four layers had pants and were white silk, a light blue silk, a dark blue cotton, then a quilted silk of darker blue. The fifth and sixth layers consisted of two long white robes. The seventh layer was the ceremonial dress of white silk embroidered with gold and silver. On the four corners of the robe and on each shoe I had the servants sew a pearl. These pearls were the lanterns to guide Mama into the next world.

The next day the monks came and took Mama's body, placing it on a piece of wood. Then, they transferred the body to a coffin. They left the sealed coffin in the house for over one hundred days and filled the house with their chanting.

After my mother died, my father said he could no longer feel joy. My parents had been promised to each other since my father's birth, and had lived a long and happy life together. How could my father live without my mother? A hundred days after her death, he died of grief.

With both our parents gone, my brothers, sisters and I felt abandoned. Your grandfather said to me, "Now there is no one in the world who can scold us or tell us right from wrong."

Hsü Chih-mo did not appear at any of the ceremonies for my parents. I had not expected him to appear for my sake, only out of respect for my brothers. None of them, however, seemed insulted by Hsü Chih-mo's absence. Second Brother had written me when I was in Sawston that the news of the divorce was as tragic to him as the death of our parents. Second Brother loved Hsü Chih-mo as much as he loved our parents. Of course he would forgive Hsü Chih-mo's absence at the funerals.

CHAPTER THIRTEEN

A PERSON'S TITLE

Yu-i did not admit it to me, but I suspect that she was thrilled to be needed by the Hsü family, to return to China in such a valuable position. She did not seem as bitter about Hsü Chih-mo's new wife, Lu Xiaoman, as she was about Lin Huiyin. I was glad of this.

I understood what Yu-i meant when she said she felt uneducated and illiterate compared to Lu Xiaoman. Yu-i expressed herself in actions more than words and seemed to proceed through life in a much less self-conscious manner than Hsü Chih-mo and Lu Xiaoman. She said that she had kept a diary the entire time she was in Germany but burned it when Hsü Chih-mo and Lu Xiaoman published their own diaries in 1927. Yu-i did not want anyone to get hold of hers and publish it alongside theirs!

Lu Xiaoman's diary seemed so inspiring to me. If I had been Hsü Chih-mo, I would have felt that I was indeed changing China by igniting this woman with my love.

As a romantic poet, Tagore's interpreter and Lu Xiaoman's ardent suitor, Hsü Chih-mo became a national celebrity. His works, which ranged from eulogies for writers such as Thomas Hardy and Katherine Mansfield to essays on artistic development, gained a large popular following.

A contemporary romantic poet, Yu Dafu, commented on the forbidden romance between Hsü Chih-mo and Lu Xiaoman some ten years later:

> When an honest and beautiful woman like Hsiao-man [Xiaoman] met a passionate and sincere man like Chih-mo, naturally it would set off sparks and flare into burning fire. How could they care about cardinal norms or ethical tenets? How could they care about clan laws or family convention? When the affair was becoming the butt of social gossip in Peking [Beijing], my admiration for the bravery of Hsiao-man and the sincerity of Chih-mo could not have been greater.

Hsü Chih-mo's and Lu Xiaoman's wedding was held on October 3, 1926, at the Beihai Garden in Beijing. Liang Qichao, Hsü Chih-mo's teacher, acted as master of ceremonies. He shocked the guests by delivering a speech which said that he disapproved of Hsü Chih-mo's actions and considered what the two of them were doing immoral. Liang Qichao said that both he and others had tried to persuade Hsü Chih-mo not to proceed with it, but to no avail.

"Hsü Chih-mo, you are a flighty character who has really achieved nothing. You are not really devoted to love and ideals. You had better change your ways and become a new man," Liang Qichao scolded Hsü Chih-mo.

In the middle of Liang Qichao's speech, Hsü Chih-mo stood up and said to him: "You have said enough. Please be merciful."

My grandfather, Yu-i's Eighth Brother, attended Hsü Chih-mo's wedding and spoke with me about it when he visited my parents' home in Connecticut in 1984. He told me that Hsü Chih-mo had known that Liang Qichao was going to criticize him at the wedding reception.

"Then why did Hsü Chih-mo let Liang Qichao talk?" I asked.

"First of all," my grandfather said, "it gave face to Liang Qichao, letting him air his views like that."

I agreed with him.

"Then," my grandfather suggested, "it gave face to the Chang family."

I said I doubted that Hsü Chih-mo had given thought to that idea. In fact, I thought that the main reason Hsü Chih-mo had allowed Liang Qichao to speak was to highlight the iconoclastic nature of his own actions.

My grandfather looked annoyed with me. He said that I did not show enough respect for Hsü Chih-mo, that I had to try to understand him better. Hsü Chih-mo brought great honor to the Chang family with his talent.

For my part, I was bothered by my grandfather's unadulterated admiration for Hsü Chih-mo. He seemed to appreciate Hsü Chih-mo more than he did his own sister. During my grandfather's visit East, he stayed with us in Connecticut. Yu-i had always been comfortable at our house but, with my grandfather there, she seemed stiff and formal. When she spoke, she sounded strident, more forceful than normal, as if concerned that my grandfather would question or ridicule her authority. And, indeed, he did tend to treat some of her remarks as trivial.

Their styles clashed terribly, I thought. My grandfather's usually playful and joking manner—which everyone in the family said most resembled Hsü Chih-mo's personality—seemed squashed by Yu-i's seriousness. I bet this was often the dynamic between Yu-i and Hsü Chih-mo. On his deathbed in 1985, my grandfather admonished me "to be kind to Hsü Chih-mo" in my studies and writings, and requested a reading of Hsü Chih-mo's poetry at his own funeral.

Nearly five months passed between my abrupt departure from Beijing to Mama's bedside in Shanghai and the last day of mourning for Baba. Gone from Beijing for so long, I canceled the lease on the house and placed A-huan in school in Shanghai.

After the funerals, I decided that it was better not to change his school again. I wanted to stay in Shanghai but could not afford to live in Shanghai proper. The financial burden of the entire family now rested on Fourth Brother, and he agreed with me that it would be too expensive for me and the younger siblings to continue living in the family house in Shanghai. Fourth Brother had actually been paying the rent on the house for Mama and Baba, but the funeral expenses had set him back, and he wished to relinquish the lease.

I still had my three hundred dollars a month from the Hsü family. I told Fourth Brother that I could take the little ones and live in the countryside. He agreed. Fourth Sister, Eighth Brother, A-huan and I moved out to a small town about a half-hour train ride from Shanghai. I paid for the rent and food. Fourth Sister got her pocket money from First Sister and her husband, who were living in the city. They also let her stay with them sometimes. Eighth Brother, who was twenty-four, and at his first job at a bank, commuted back and forth each day with A-huan.

At that time Fourth Brother was living with his wife in the city. They had a lovely home in one of the foreign concessions, where it was considered very prestigious for Chinese to live. Fourth Brother was general manager at the Bank of China, not yet president.

One night, very late, Mama's spirit appeared in his bedroom. She floated above him, wraithlike and wrathful, in her seven layers of robes. Sensing her presence, Fourth Brother and his wife awoke. Mama's spirit pulled back the bedcovers, so that Fourth Brother and his wife lay shivering before her in cold and fear.

"How could you leave the little ones all alone like that in the countryside?" Mama's spirit scolded Fourth Brother. "You were supposed to take care of them! You're the one in charge!"

Do you remember how I told you about the Light World and the Shadow World, that when people die they pass from one to the other? I had never talked to my mother about my divorce before her death, and believe that she returned from the Shadow World primarily because she worried about me.

Fourth Brother also thought that this was Mama's message to him, because he called me the next day and offered me his house. He insisted that Mama's spirit would rest only if I took his house. He and his wife, who was very superstitious, would move out immediately.

Three years later, in return for the house he gave me, I helped Fourth Brother buy another home of his own in the French concession. But I took over the title deed to the house at 125 Avenue Hague located in the "Fan Yuan" compound. "Fan" was the man who had owned the land before British control. "Yuan" meant garden. In the middle of the compound, which consisted of about ten houses, was a huge flower garden complete with paths and fountains. My new house was located toward the rear of the compound and was made of stone. It had three bedrooms, a kitchen, servants' quarters and a terrace off the living room.

I made a quick tour of the downstairs and then headed for the master bedroom at the top of the stairs. I sat very still on the edge of the large bed and closed my eyes. After a long moment I thought I heard a sound.

"Mama?" I called softly.

A tree branch rubbed against the window. I did not move.

"Mama?" I called again, this time a little louder. Then I felt her spirit in the room, like a strange gust of air. I was not frightened at all. I told Mama that we little ones were fine. She could return to the Shadow World and rest there in peace.

After settling into my new home, I began to look around for a job as a teacher. I taught one semester of German at Dongwu University, and was considering teaching a second, when some women from the Shanghai Women's Savings Bank approached me. I think that Fourth Brother, fulfilling his duty to Mama to look after me, had sent them around to me. The women said they wanted me to work at their bank because I knew a lot of people and could use the influence of Fourth Brother—general manager of the Bank of China and the founder of *Bankers Weekly*, a reference volume on Chinese and economic problems—to secure money. They had to be honest with me about my connections being more important than my ability; I had never before worked at a bank.

Although teaching was my training, I decided to seize the opportunity. But I said that I would only become vice-president of the bank, not president. I thought, how would that look if my brother became president of one bank and I was the president of another?

The people who ran the bank before me had given away all the money to friends, relatives, or anyone who asked, and now the bank was almost penniless. They wanted me to try to save it.

"Don't hire any lawyers," I told the women at the bank. "We're poor enough already." I said that I would talk to each of the debtors, try to work with them and see if together we could figure out a way for them to return payment.

The bank had been founded in 1910 for women by women,

and was located in the center of town on Nanjing East Road. It was popular with both the older women and the younger women. The young women, many of whom worked in nearby stores, liked to cash their paychecks with us and leave a little money immediately in their accounts as savings. This way, they did not have to worry about budgeting their money, spending it all on Western clothing, silk stockings and lipsticks. And when they were married and stopped working, they could have a little sum of money on their own free from their husbands.

Most of the older women used the bank to store jewelry they could not keep at a husband's bank. These were mainly gifts from boyfriends. For example, before any major social event, all the other banks were extremely busy as huge cars would drive to the door and rich women would emerge to retrieve their necklaces or headpieces for the party. The Women's Bank, however, was never as busy at these times, for we were the guardians of the more unofficial pieces of jewelry, and these were retrieved for different occasions.

I had my desk placed at the back of the bank so that I could see everyone and everything in front of me. I liked to arrive at the office each morning exactly at nine o'clock. This was a habit that I learned in Germany, to be very punctual. I was always on time. People would come in late, see me and apologize. I would tell them not to worry about it.

Every day at five o'clock a Chinese tutor arrived at the office for me. I told you this before: I had stopped studying formally at the age of fifteen and felt that I needed to learn more about literature and the classics.

After an hour or so with the tutor, I would head over on Nanjing East Road to the dress shop that I managed. Located on Shanghai's most fashionable street, this dress shop was a little project between Eighth Brother and a few friends, including Hsü Chih-mo. Eighth Brother had conceived the idea for the store: a combination of ready-made and made-to-order clothing. We displayed samples in the shop and would then alter these samples to fit the woman's taste and exact size. Our fancy beading, buttons and ribbon work became so distinctive, the customer could brag, "I got this at Yunchang."

Naming the store Yunchang, which means "Cloud and Clothing," Eighth Brother alluded to a poem by the eighth-century poet Li Bo, about the Emperor's Precious Consort Yang:

> *One sees her dress, so like the cloud;*
> *Her face, the flower.*

I was Yunchang's general manager, which meant that I checked the orders and talked to the tailor at the end of the day, just to keep an eye on things.

When I got home I would help A-huan with his studies, try to go over what he did not know. Three times a week, beginning at eight in the evening, I would play mah-jongg. I still play now a few times a week.

I even began to entertain for Fourth Brother and Second Brother at my home, which they preferred over restaurants. Each brother had his own house and own wife who could entertain for him, but they liked to use my house. Fourth Brother's wife preferred to spend her evenings with mah-jongg and opium, and Second Brother's wife did not like the disruption caused by the endless stream of people who wanted to speak with Second Brother. She once said to him, "How can the servants do any work if they are always serving your friends?"

Knowing her opinion, Second Brother once asked me in amazement, "Why don't you complain about all the people who come to visit me?"

I said to him, "It's your business to talk with others. If people don't come over all the time, then this means that you're not doing well in your business."

In 1934, Second Brother appointed me the treasurer of his political party, the National Socialist. People always ask me about this position, but I tell them that I think Second Brother just wanted to be able to say, "I'll have to check with my treasurer," so that he did not have to give out money all the time.

Not long after I moved into Fan Yuan, and about a half year after his wedding, Hsü Chih-mo and Lu Xiaoman rented a house on Avenue Édouard VII in the French concession. Lao Ye and Lao Taitai moved from Xiashi to the city, because it was safer in the city at the time with the warlords fighting. Even after the initial difficulties involving the red sedan chair, rice and the staircase, the elder Hsüs lived together with Hsü Chih-mo and Lu Xiaoman. This living arrangement, where the married couple live with the son's parents, is the usual Chinese way. Depending on the season and regional political skirmishes, Lao Ye and Lao Taitai would go back and forth for months at a time between Shanghai and Xiashi.

The French concession, where Hsü Chih-mo rented for a while, was a very fancy area like the British concession. There was the Cercle Sportif Français, a sports club that the French went to, and the French Park, with a large stone inside named for a French aviator. On Saturdays, I would take A-huan through the shaded streets of the concession to Hsü Chih-mo's home, so that A-huan could spend time with his grandparents. Since the Hsüs had raised A-huan the first seven years of his life, they were very close. Lao Ye would buy toys for A-huan from one of the modern stores along Nanjing Road; Lao Taitai had the servants prepare special foods for him. A-huan always returned from these visits happy and full.

One afternoon I ran into Hsü Chih-mo when I was dropping A-huan off at their home.

Hsü Chih-mo stopped me. "I've been thinking," he said anxiously. "What do you think A-huan should call Lu Xiaoman?"

In China a person's title is very important because it reflects the level of respect due that person. While I always took care to address others correctly, Hsü Chih-mo had seemingly renounced these traditions long ago. Why should he care now, I thought grudgingly.

"What about Ji Mu?" Hsü Chih-mo asked me, using the word for "adopted mother" or "stepmother."

I said, as dispassionately as possible, "Whatever you like, as long as A-huan is willing to call her that."

But when Hsü Chih-mo tried "Ji Mu" on A-huan, who was nearly ten years old then, A-huan refused. He did not want to call Lu Xiaoman anything.

I myself have nothing against Lu Xiaoman. When she and Hsü Chih-mo fell in love, it was none of my business; I was already divorced from him. In fact, I was happy for her that she was able to get a divorce from her first husband so that she could marry Hsü Chih-mo. But her divorce was different from mine because by the time she got it, some three years after mine, divorce for free love was becoming fashionable in China. Also, Lu Xiaoman already had someone else to turn to after her divorce; I had had only myself to fall back on.

During the years when we were all neighbors in Shanghai, I had dinner with Lu Xiaoman only once. We were both guests at Hu Shi's home. He had been the one sending Hsü Chih-mo letters in Italy. Later they worked together on a progressive literary journal, the *Crescent Moon Monthly*. When Hu Shi invited me to dinner, he asked if I would be willing to come even if Lu Xiaoman were there.

I said, "Of course. It doesn't matter to me." I was divorced; I had no ties to Hsü Chih-mo, as much as I was involved with his family.

I do not know exactly why Hu Shi was so intent on bringing Lu Xiaoman and me together, but I felt I could not refuse. Maybe he was out to show how progressive we had all become, or maybe he was just interested in what might happen. Either way, I knew I had to show my *zhiqi*, my dignity, by going. Also, I had heard that Hu Shi himself was in love with Lu Xiaoman. His own wife was old-fashioned, with bound feet. He had studied in America but returned to marry her.

At dinner that night, I realized just how beautiful Lu Xiaoman was. Her skin was lustrous and her features very fine. All the men were captivated when she spoke. During the meal she called Hsü Chih-mo "Mo" and "Mo Mo," a diminutive of "Chih-mo." He called her "Man" and "May," an endearment of "Xiaoman." He spoke to her with such patience, such respect. All of this I observed, and re-membered that, with me, Hsü Chih-mo had always been short, curt.

I said little that night, but did not betray my feelings. I knew I was not charming, not like other women. I got hard because my life went that way.

One day I received a telephone call from Lao Taitai. She said to me, "I can't stand it anymore. I must tell you about Lu Xiaoman. I can-not bear to live in the same household with this woman any longer.

"There is a man named Mr. Weng here," Lao Taitai said. "Lu Xiaoman met him through her friends in the opera, and he is now her boyfriend. He has started living here.

"There was a ham in the icebox, and I had the servants heat it up for Lao Ye and me for dinner. The next day Lu Xiaoman opened the icebox and wanted to know where her ham was. I told her that Lao Ye and I had eaten it. She turned to me and screamed, scolding me, 'Why did you do that? That ham was especially prepared for Mr. Weng!'

"I don't understand it," Lao Taitai continued. "Hsü Chih-mo doesn't seem to mind that Mr. Weng is here. He came home from Beijing so tired, with a sore throat, after many hours of teaching. I told the servants to prepare some ginseng medicine for him because there was some excellent ginseng in the cupboard. But then the servants said to me that we couldn't touch the ginseng in the house because it was reserved for Mr. Weng!

"Who belongs here?" Lao Taitai exclaimed. "The parents, the daughter-in-law or the boyfriend, Mr. Weng? Hsü Chih-mo doesn't care at all. He said that as long as Lu Xiaoman and Mr. Weng were lying together on the hookah bed sharing their opium, there was nothing wrong. 'They are sharing each other's company,' Hsü Chih-mo said. But last night when he came home, he crawled up on the other side of the hookah bed to be with Lu Xiaoman. Lu Xiaoman and Mr. Weng must have been doing opium all night because I found all three of them there this morning, curled up on the hookah bed together: Mr. Weng and Lu Xiaoman around the hookah, then Hsü Chih-mo on the other side of Lu Xiaoman with hardly any room, almost falling off the bed.

"The family has come to ruin," Lao Taitai said. "I don't want to live here anymore. Lao Ye and I want to move in with you."

I had never heard Lao Taitai so upset. She had never before said to me that she wanted to transfer her household to mine. I knew that if Lao Ye and Lao Taitai moved in with me, fleeing Hsü Chih-mo's house directly, Lu Xiaoman would lose face. I told the Hsüs that they could live with me after they had spent about a week in Xiashi.

"Oh, I see." Lao Taitai's voice brightened. "That's what we'll do."

When the Hsüs returned from Xiashi, they told Hsü Chih-mo that they were going to spend a little time with their grandson. They ended up staying for many years. Either Hsü Chih-mo did not see through this approach, or he chose to say nothing.

Apparently, Lu Xiaoman had met her boyfriend, Weng Ruiwu, several months after marrying Hsü Chih-mo. The occasion was a two-day Beijing opera performance organized by Hsü Chih-mo's artist friend, Jiang Xiaojian. Lu Xiaoman and Mr. Weng, a famous Beijing opera star, played the leading parts, Hsü Chih-mo, a supporting role. Through the performance the three became good friends. After the performance Lu Xiaoman fell sick because of fatigue, and Mr. Weng offered her massage services. Hsü Chih-mo did not object; in fact, Mr. Weng spent so much time at their house, the three became even closer friends. Mr. Weng actually came from a very good family. His father, a provincial official in the former Qing bureaucracy, was well versed in painting and collected fine art. And, through ancestral inheritance, Mr. Weng owned a mountain that produced a regular harvest of tea. Later, however, Mr. Weng introduced Lu Xiaoman to opium smoking, and eventually she became addicted.

It is terrible, this addiction, and I felt sorry for Lu Xiaoman. When I was about fourteen and with the family on vacation in Hangzhou, Fourth Sister and I ate several bowls apiece of unclean shrimp—live tender ones from the West Lake with hot oil poured over them—and fell ill with stomach cramps and fever. Baba said it was typhoid and wanted to give us some opium to calm us. Fourth Sister took a small amount and was quiet immediately. But when Baba came to me I turned my head and refused.

"What will happen to me if I become addicted to it?" I asked my father. "Will you always be here to take care of me and buy me opium if I need it?"

My father thought I was disturbed by the illness and did not answer me.

"So I will bear the pain," I said because already then I knew about opium. People smoked on the hookah bed and the smoke traveled upward; even rats got addicted to the stuff, and gathered on the rafters whenever the hookah was lit. Even though Fourth Sister was only about two, she grew to like it, and cried for days when Baba would not give it to her. The only reason she did not become addicted was because she was young, and Baba had given her only a little bit. But I was much older than she and did not want to take the risk.

After I made some money in the stock market I built a separate house for Lao Ye and Lao Taitai on an empty lot behind my own house. The two houses were only a few hundred yards apart: the back door of their new house faced the back door of my house. But I thought it was important that my in-laws lived separate from me because Hsü Chih-mo and I were divorced.

Still, the traffic was heavy between our houses. Sometimes Lao Ye and Lao Taitai might have dinner with me, or I might send A-huan to keep them company at their new house. As the years went by, people would say that Lao Ye and Lao Taitai were so disappointed in Hsü Chih-mo that they ousted him and grew to love me more. But I never believed that. How could a family abandon its only son? How could they ever love me more than him? The parents just did not understand Hsü Chih-mo because they were of the old school.

Life is very strange. Here I was a divorced woman, divorced from my husband because he thought that the two of us were incompatible, and I actually got along with him better after our divorce than during our marriage.

Hsü Chih-mo usually lectured on art and literature in Beijing but commuted from Shanghai because Lu Xiaoman preferred to live there. I saw Hsü Chih-mo practically every day when he was in Shanghai. He and I actually became close to each other after the divorce. He used to come visit at the dress shop. If he was going to go on a trip, he would come to me to order shirts or pants. One time I made him a tie. Then he came back and told me that he had lost it, and we had to make him another.

In the summer of 1928, Hsü Chih-mo went to Europe on a lecture tour. Lao Ye and Lao Taitai were living in the countryside of Xiashi at the time. One day, shortly after Hsü Chih-mo left, Lao Ye took the train into the city and went especially to see Lu Xiaoman. He decided that, with Hsü Chih-mo gone for so long, he would try to be friendly with Lu Xiaoman.

"It is unnecessary for you to keep a big house all to yourself like that," he said. "Why don't you put the car in the garage, keep only one servant to look after the house while you are gone and come stay with us in the country?"

Lao Ye was trying to save money, and also to give Lu Xiaoman a chance to save face with him and Lao Taitai. He went back to the country to wait for Lu Xiaoman to appear. She never replied or showed up in Xiashi. When Hsü Chih-mo returned to China in January 1929, Lao Ye met him at the train station.

"I have decided that I will no longer speak to your wife. If she is going to ignore me, then why should I try to be kind to her?" Lao Ye announced to Hsü Chih-mo.

Afterward, when Lao Ye and Lao Taitai were in the city, Hsü Chih-mo came alone to see his parents. He tried on occasion to bring Lu Xiaoman, but Lao Ye would see their car approaching and run out of his house to my house. He would slip out the back door of his house and cross the yard to mine, leaving Lao Taitai on her own to greet the couple.

Then, after Hsü Chih-mo and Lu Xiaoman left, Lao Ye would hurry back to his own house so that he could learn from Lao Taitai how the two of them were getting along. This is how much Lao Ye loved his son.

If the parents wanted a daughter-in-law, I always did right. I wonder if I could have done anything differently. But when I treated my in-laws well, I thought, they are the grandparents of my son. How could I be bad to them?

But sometimes it was difficult to stand in between Hsü Chih-mo and his parents. I did not know where I fit in the family, what I was supposed to do when Lao Taitai fell seriously ill with asthma in 1930. Lao Ye called Hsü Chih-mo in Shanghai and told him that he had to get to Xiashi. Then Lao Ye called me and said that I had to go also. I was horrified to hear that Lao Taitai was gravely ill, and I wanted to go to her bedside immediately, but I knew that Hsü Chih-mo and Lu Xiaoman were going, and I did not want to be in the same house with Lu Xiaoman. Also, I believed that, in big matters such as a death, I had to stand firm on my position in the family: I was divorced.

I told Lao Ye that I would send A-huan to Xiashi. A-huan and Hsü Chih-mo met at the train station and traveled together to the countryside.

That afternoon Lao Ye called again and asked me why I still had not come. I finally said to him, "I am divorced. I should not interfere with the affairs of the house."

I said this because it was Lu Xiaoman's duty to take care of the in-laws, not mine, and I didn't want Hsü Chih-mo or her to be angry with me for interfering.

Late in the night Lao Ye called yet again. He sounded frantic. "You must come to the house at once. There is no woman in the house. We do not know what to do."

"Why me?" I answered. "I am divorced. I said to Lao Ye, "You get Hsü Chih-mo on the phone." Hsü Chih-mo appeared at the other end and said frantically, "I can't do anything; she is so sick. I don't know the medicine."

I thought for a long moment. "You people are very selfish," I said at long last. "Now that you need me, you ask me to come. If Lu Xiaoman also comes to the house, then what shall I do? How will it look with two women under the same roof? Also, will I be allowed to stay for the ceremonies? How will that look?"

I had to stand firm with the family because this was a big matter. "If I come," I said, "I will not leave the house when Lu Xiaoman arrives. I must be allowed to stay for the ceremonies."

Hsü Chih-mo sounded desperate and beaten. "Okay, okay, you just come," he said.

I arrived at the house about two weeks before Lao Taitai died. She was very weak, but she expressed how happy she was that I had come. Now she knew everything would be done correctly.

I did all the work of the main wife for the funeral. I was the one who put the cloth pack in Lao Taitai's mouth and then hired someone to dress her in the different layers, sew on the pearls, then pack her body into the coffin. I summoned the monks for weeks of continuous prayer, the tailors for preparation of the white sackcloth funeral garments. Then I hired the crier who stood by the coffin during the ceremony and wailed loudly each time a friend or relative made his obeisance to the deceased. Three deep bows upon walking up to the coffin, three deep bows upon leaving the coffin, I taught A-huan, who was then twelve.

Lu Xiaoman arrived in Xiashi the morning of the funeral, and secluded herself in the bedroom at the main house until the actual ceremony. Knowing she would come, I had been staying in the old family house with the uncle and cousins. I would not stay in the same house with Lu Xiaoman.

But she and I were both at Lao Taitai's funeral. Lao Ye, the chief mourner, stood at the side of the coffin, bowing to people as they stepped forward to pay their respects to Lao Taitai's body. Dressed in white sackcloth and with my head bowed, I took my place next to Hsü Chih-mo, Lu Xiaoman and A-huan, as the adopted daughter of the Hsü family.

CHAPTER FOURTEEN

THE END OF
MY STORY

In the spring of 1986, I went to Shanghai in search of Yu-i's past. I wanted to see the streets she had walked on, the house she had lived in, the space she had moved in. It was getting so I could barely visit her in New York without having her past and her story overwhelm me. I could not see the eighty-six-year-old woman who rose every day, did her exercises, took her vitamins and faced the day with fresh resolve. When I was with her, I could see nothing but her past: disjointed images, fragmented abstractions, recurring themes and everything in terms of Hsü Chih-mo, Lu Xiaoman, Lin Huiyin, Berlin and Shanghai.

I did not understand all of the story. Yu-i made Hsü Chih-mo sound so heroic. In the beginning, she maintained that he divorced her because of a girlfriend, but by the end she said he divorced her because he respected women and did not want to see them compromised. Which was the truth? Had Yu-i taken her anger toward Hsü Chih-mo and twisted it into love and gratitude?

Her interpretation of the divorce troubled me even as I left her behind in New York and flew to Shanghai. There I met up with a son of Fourth Brother's, who still remembered the old places. With a car and driver, we started the morning along the Bund, the magnificent tree-lined boulevard that ran the length of the Huangpu River on the eastern edge of the city. Now called Zhongshan Dong Road (after Sun Yat-sen), this road was and still is Shanghai's main thoroughfare. We passed the People's Park, formerly a British park whose sign had supposedly read: NO CHINESE OR DOGS ALLOWED. We continued along the Bund and saw the Bank of China where Fourth Brother had once been president, and next door, the Sassoon House where he had taken his afternoon naps.

All the street names were different now, and I sat with a map spread across my knees and a bottle of whiteout in one hand, crossing out the harsh x's and z's of pinyin romanization and Communist street names. In their place I drew in foreign settlement lines and wrote in road names like Lafayette and Bubbling Well and Joffre. Over the Shanghai Municipal Library and People's Park and Square, I drew in the club and racecourse that had marked the corners of the British and French Settlements.

Thanks to my uncle, to whom only directions and twists of the old roads mattered—not names—we found the dress store that was now a copy shop, and the bank Yu-i presided over that was now a hardware store. Leaving the center of town with its throng of bicycles, we made our way to the residential part of town where buildings were set back from the wide streets and lined by sloping curved walls. My uncle pointed out a small house in the French concession on Avenue Édouard VII where Hsü Chih-mo and Lu Xiaoman lived for a while; they were renting, he said. And I sat with the map of Shanghai and drew in a big *H* for Hsü Chih-mo amid the *Y*'s for Yu-i.

Finally we were at Yu-i's home in the former British concession. It was now a military hospital of some sort. Standing in the grounds of Fan Yuan, I could still sense the grace of the past, the beckoning willow trees, the artistry of the landscaping. One ally that I had not counted on was the almost eerie timelessness of Shanghai.

Somehow, the ghosts of the past had not yet vanished, and on that morning their presence grew stronger, transporting me back several decades. Walking Yu-i's very steps in Fan Yuan, I understood the need to accept her story as she had willed it to me.

The last time I saw Hsü Chih-mo was the day before he died in 1931. He came around to the store to say hello to Eighth Brother and to ask me about some shirts that he wanted the tailor to make for him. He had just flown into Shanghai for the day to show a friend's house that was for sale. Hsü Chih-mo was acting as broker; if he sold the house for his friend, he got a commission.

Hsü Chih-mo always flew even though airplane travel at that time was still dangerous. The foreign firms were safer than the Chinese ones, but Hsü Chih-mo said that he was flying China Airlines because he had a book of free passes. One of Hsü Chih-mo's most famous essays was about flying, and the company wanted to use him as part of their advertising campaign.

That afternoon he said that he had to return to Beijing immediately. I asked why he had to rush; he could go back the next day. I also told him that I did not think that he should fly China Airlines, free or not. He laughed like he always did and told me that he would be fine.

That evening I played mah-jongg at a friend's house and came home late. I was only half asleep at one or two in the morning when a servant came in and told me that a man from the Bank of China was at the door trying to deliver a telegram to me.

En route to Beijing, Hsü Chih-mo's China Airlines charter plane had crashed in Ji'nan, Shandong Province, the telegram said.

Hsü Chih-mo, the sole passenger, and the two pilots had died instantly.

I stood in the hallway in my robe in complete disbelief. I had just seen Hsü Chih-mo alive.

"What do we do?" the man from the bank prompted me. "I have been to Hsü Chih-mo's home, but Lu Xiaoman will not take this telegram. She says it isn't true that Hsü Chih-mo is dead. She refuses to claim his body."

I imagined Lu Xiaoman closing the front door and disappearing in a cloud of opium. What was wrong with her? How could Lu Xiaoman refuse to take responsibility for Hsü Chih-mo's body? From that time, I never believed in the kind of love that Hsü Chih-mo and Lu Xiaoman shared.

I told the messenger to come into the dining room. A servant brought him tea, while I collected my thoughts. A-huan, as Hsü Chih-mo's son, had to go to identify his father's body. Someone, but not I—it should have been Lu Xiaoman—had to go with thirteen-year-old A-huan to handle the funeral arrangements.

I called up Eighth Brother. He began sobbing on the telephone when I told him the news.

"Would you be able to take A-huan to Ji'nan tomorrow?" I asked him.

"Of course, of course," he just managed to say.

The next morning, when Lao Ye came to breakfast, I told him that there had been an airplane crash. I did not have to say who. Of all the people we knew, only Hsü Chih-mo flew regularly.

He asked me the condition of the passenger. I did not dare tell Lao Ye the truth immediately; I was afraid it would shock him at his old age. So I pretended that Hsü Chih-mo was still alive. I said he was in the hospital and that it looked very bad.

Lao Ye said he would not visit the hospital to see his son in such condition. I was to go and report back to him.

The next day at breakfast Lao Ye asked me, "What's the news?" I looked down at my plate and said, "They are trying, but I don't know what they can do."

The following day Lao Ye asked for news again. Then, finally, I told him, crying as I did, because it was as if I was hearing the news for the first time again. "There is no hope. He is gone."

I saw so much on Lao Ye's face then: grief, sorrow, regret. He turned away from me and said, "Okay. So, forget it." *Suy le va.*

It was a terrible thing to say, but he was so hurt by Hsü Chih-mo, and angry at him after he married Lu Xiaoman.

A search party was sent to the mountainside to sift through the wreckage of the plane. Hsü Chih-mo's body was found not far from the crash site. The corpse was mutilated and badly burned, but still recognizable.

His body was kept up in Ji'nan, and the Bank of China officiated over a preliminary memorial and funeral service for him there. A-huan and Eighth Brother attended, and Lao Ye mourned Hsü Chih-mo properly by composing a poem for the occasion. In his poem, he boldly compared Hsü Chih-mo to several famous poets: Qu Yuan, who in the third century B.C. had drowned himself in the River Xiang because his ruler no longer trusted him, and the Tang poet, Li Bo, who was said to have drowned in a drunken attempt to seize the moon's reflection.

> *History shows me poets*
> *Drowning in the Xiang or*
> *Seizing the moon in the water;*

> *Men of letters untimely dead.*
> *But how to foretell the tragedy*
> *Of you, soaring one,*
> *Caught unaware by that brutal wind?*
>
> *From times in the cradle,*
> *Through schooldays and learning with masters,*
> *Your father and mother always made sure*
> *You received the best.*
> *You were our only son, our dearest one.*
> *Now, with your mother gone,*
> *Your father in lonely grief*
> *Makes these verses to summon your soul.*

I wanted to say something at the memorial also. But I did not know how to begin expressing my grief. One of Second Brother's friends wrote a poem under my name, calling upon the Peng bird from the Ji'nan area whose back is countless leagues broad and migrates every year to the Pool of Heaven.

> *Ten thousand miles away, soaring like the famed bird of Peng*
> *In the misty clouds. Alas! You lost your way!*
> *We learn, in shock, you had become a crane;*
> *Your young son must go summoning your soul—how very sad!*

Six months after Hsü Chih-mo's death and the memorial service, the Bank of China finally managed to arrange a train car to take Hsü Chih-mo's body from Ji'nan to Shanghai en route to Xiashi for burial. Travel was difficult then because of the fighting going on between the Nationalists and the Japanese in that area. Eighth Brother took A-huan to receive the sealed coffin in Shanghai.

I did not even plan to go to the service in Shanghai, but I prepared a black cheongsam just in case. That afternoon the telephone rang in the house.

"You must come," a friend said.

I asked why.

"You just come," he said. So I went to the funeral hall where Hsü Chih-mo's casket had been opened and placed among flowers. Against his dark silk robe, his face looked all powdery white and swollen, nothing like him. I bowed three times very deeply to show my respect. He had been only thirty-five, so young and talented.

After I stepped away from the coffin the friend who had called me to the hall appeared next to me, relieved. "You have to help," he insisted. "Lu Xiaoman wants to change Hsü Chih-mo's clothes to a Western suit, and she does not like the coffin either. She wants a Western one."

With the Bank of China's help, Eighth Brother had arranged for Hsü Chih-mo's coffin to be made of the traditional *shou ban*, longevity boards, which were rounded on one side. The coffin resembled the trunk of a tree, not a rectangular box.

I felt disgusted at the thought of moving Hsü Chih-mo's body from one setting to another. Also his clothing. How could his body possibly be subjected to more abuse?

"Even if he had died of natural causes," I said, "it would be difficult to change everything now. But Hsü Chih-mo died such an unnatural death . . ."

I did not want to see Lu Xiaoman, to talk to her, and have to fight with her. "You just tell Lu Xiaoman that I said no," I finished.

I left then, just in case Lu Xiaoman appeared. Later, I heard that they did leave Hsü Chih-mo in Chinese clothes and a Chinese coffin. I did not understand Lu Xiaoman. Was Hsü Chih-mo so Western that he needed to be in Western clothing at his death? I did not think so.

No matter how Western or progressive his thoughts, I believed Hsü Chih-mo to be Chinese, for the Western love that he sought did not save him in the end. Only last year, I read his letters to Lu Xiaoman before his death. Hsü Chih-mo never had a family life with her. She refused to move to Beijing because opium was more readily available in Shanghai, and Hsü Chih-mo was always flying between Beijing and Shanghai trying to support her. Reading about his life at the end makes me so sad.

Do you know why Hsü Chih-mo was flying the night that he died? He was hurrying back to Beijing to attend a lecture on architecture given by Lin Huiyin, his girlfriend when he divorced me. Still Lin Huiyin in the end, from the Sawston days, through their Tagore tour together, even after her marriage to Liang Sicheng. She, Hsü Chih-mo and even the husband were good friends. By chance, Liang Sicheng was visiting Shandong Province when Hsü Chih-mo's plane crashed there. He and his friends were in the first of the search parties.

I met Lin Huiyin once in 1947, when I was in Beijing for a wedding. A friend came to me and said that Lin Huiyin was in the hospital. She had just undergone a serious operation for tuberculosis and could die. Even her husband, Liang Sicheng, had been summoned back from the States, Yale University, where he was teaching. Why did Lin Huiyin want to see me? I thought. But I went with A-huan and the grandchildren. She was too weak to say anything, just looked at us and turned her head here and there. She studied me closely, though. I do not know what she wanted to see. Maybe that I was ugly and could not smile.

As it turned out, Lin Huiyin did not die till 1954, of tuberculosis. I think she asked to see me that time, though, because she loved Hsü Chih-mo and wanted to see his children. Even though she was married to Liang, she still loved Hsü Chih-mo. But if Lin Huiyin loved Hsü Chih-mo, why did she leave him hanging after the divorce? Was that love?

They said that Lu Xiaoman, the second wife, loved Hsü Chih-mo. But if I look at the way she acted at his death—not claiming his body—that was not love. How could you refuse to take care of another? Love means taking responsibility, fulfilling a duty.

And the two of them had no family life together. Lu Xiaoman's opium addiction made Hsü Chih-mo very poor. He always had to ask his friends for money. He would ask me for money, and if I gave him some from my own pocket, I would say, "It's from your father."

Hsü Chih-mo himself had no bad habits. He did not drink, he did not smoke opium. He did not even start smoking cigarettes until about a year or so before his death. He had a wonderful personality. In any society, he would have been loved.

My entire life, I have worried about fulfilling my duty. Even after the divorce I took care of Hsü Chih-mo's parents because I thought it was my responsibility to do so. I did what I thought was right for Hsü Chih-mo, his family and son.

When Hsü Chih-mo was alive Lao Ye helped support him with three hundred dollars each month. After Hsü Chih-mo's death Lao Ye kept giving Lu Xiaoman three hundred dollars a month, because he thought it was his duty to take care of her. He had the three hundred dollars deposited directly into her bank account, so that he did not have to see her. Lao Ye outlived Hsü Chih-mo by thirteen years, and during all those years he lived with me, and every month helped Lu Xiaoman, even after she began living openly with her lover, Mr. Weng. Mr. Weng and Lu Xiaoman lived together without marrying for a long time until Mr. Weng died in 1961, six years before Lu Xiaoman. All this time Mr. Weng was married; I feel so sorry for his wife and his daughters.

After Lao Ye died in 1944, I continued putting three hundred dollars a month into Lu Xiaoman's account because I thought it was my son's duty to provide for her. About four or five years later Mr. Weng came to see me. He told me he had sold several ton-bags of tea and was now wealthy enough to support Lu Xiaoman on his own. After that I stopped sending money.

Now I come to the end of my story, and in a way it is you: you are the end of my story. You are the first person to whom I ever told my entire life story. But you were interested, you wanted to know, and that is really all I have to give you, my story. You always ask me if I have time for another interview. All I have is time now, time to sit and think about the old days.

I sometimes feel that I have done everything for my family, and then for the Hsü family, because I was always concerned about what was right and what was wrong. All along, even though I was divorced, I was close to the Hsü family and even to Hsü Chih-mo. From the beginning, the fortuneteller always liked the Hsü family.

You ask me how I could run a bank, a dress shop, and still be so obedient to the Hsüs and Hsü Chih-mo. I thought that I had a duty to the Hsüs because they were my son's grandparents, and therefore my elders. I grew up with these traditional values; I could not discard them, no matter how Western I became.

So I want to thank Hsü Chih-mo for the divorce. Without it, I might never have been able to find myself, to grow. He freed me to become someone.

I read an article in a newspaper from Taiwan the other week about a man who had eighteen wives. He said that it was perfectly fine; what was there to get upset about? And he gave such good reasons. He said that all his wives were gainfully employed, had enough to eat, had their own independence. What problem was it to anyone? He explained it so clearly, saying that these reasons fulfilled any religion. Why should there be a law against polygamy?

Everyone was happy. None of the wives complained. Except the nineteenth. He was about to marry number nineteen when her mother got upset and leaked the story to the newspaper. This kind of stuff, I find so interesting, you know. It really makes you wonder about what is right and what is wrong.

I lived in Shanghai for nearly twenty years after Hsü Chih-mo's death, during which time China fought against the Japanese until 1945, and then against the Communists until 1949. When Chiang Kai-shek, the President of the ruling Kuomintang, compared the two enemies, he said that the Communists were the greater evil. The Japanese were a skin disease, while the Communists were a disease of the internal organs.

I was very lucky during this long war period: my life was not disrupted, and I made a lot of money. I bought two gross of dye that was needed for army uniforms. I waited until it was one hundred times the price and impossible to get from Germany, when I sold it. With this capital, I started investing in cotton and gold. Of all the people in the dress shop, only I made money, no one else.

One year, a woman named Mrs. Song copied every trade I made. She came over to my house every morning and called her broker right after I called mine. Now she lives in Hong Kong and she always writes me that her happiest year was with me.

The worst I ever experienced during the wars was when the Japanese invaded Shanghai in the summer of 1937, and the Women's Bank almost collapsed. This was a terrible day when the streets were filled with people fleeing the city. So many customers came in, I ran low on cash reserves and had to request a larger bank to accept the title deed of our building as collateral for a cash advance. Then a customer came into the store and wanted to withdraw all the money I had just managed to secure for our bank, forty thousand dollars.

I went in the back to the manager and said, "If this person withdraws forty thousand dollars, we cannot open the bank tomorrow. Our bank will be closed down. I want to suggest guaranteeing this amount for him. But can you guarantee it for me? Do we have enough in the safety deposit boxes?"

The manager guaranteed me that if the bank went down he would first secure my forty thousand dollars. I made him write it down. Then I went to the customer and asked if he would consider a guarantee.

Our bank was a women's bank, but this customer was a man. He said, "If you, Chang Yu-i, tell me that you guarantee it, I believe you. I would not trust anyone else's word, but yours I will trust."

We drew up an agreement that I would give him the money in six months with interest. In this way I saved our bank. I carried the guarantee on my person at all times for the next half year. In case anything happened to me, I wanted the people who found me to know my responsibility to this customer.

My son A-huan turned twenty-one in 1939. Since my return from Germany, I had watched his studies and seen that, like his father and his uncles, he was educated in both the Confucian classics and

Western learning. I did not want him to marry until he had completed his studies. When he did turn twenty-one, I asked him who he was interested in for a wife. I wanted to help him find someone suitable, not marry as I had, completely in the dark.

He said to me, "I am only interested in a beauty."

Why he responded this way, I do not understand. He reminded me of his father, who I always felt wanted someone more feminine and charming than I.

But through mah-jongg friends I heard of a beautiful young woman his age. I invited her and her mother to dinner. A-huan looked at her, spoke a few words to her, and liked her. They were married that year at a wedding of one thousand guests.

Everything has turned out well for them. They emigrated to the United States in 1947 and have lived there ever since, giving me four grandchildren, and even great-grandchildren. In the beginning, when they lived with me, I worried for my daughter-in-law. I did not want her to have the same difficulties in marriage as I had had. I offered her English, French, German and Chinese literature lessons so that she could satisfy not only A-huan's aesthetic taste but his intellectual as well.

I left Shanghai in April 1949 just a month before it fell to the Communists. Every day, on the front page of the newspaper, I would follow the map of the Communists' approach. By the time we left, there was no law and order in China. Anybody who could was fleeing. I was extremely fortunate to get a seat on an airplane. On the flight to Hong Kong, we had to watch for Communist bomber planes.

Except for First Brother, Seventh Brother, First Sister and Third Sister, all of the Chang siblings left China. We chose not to follow the Kuomintang leaders to Taiwan but to try to find a place for ourselves in the West. Most of us ended up in America, but not before we had been scattered all over the globe. Fourth Brother went first to Australia; Second Brother to Hong Kong, then India; Eighth Brother to Japan, then Brazil. All three brothers finally chose California as their home. After staying awhile in Hong Kong, Fourth Sister and I came to New York, she in 1956, and I in 1974.

In 1953, I married a man named Dr. Su. He lived downstairs from me in Hong Kong with his four teenage children. I met him through a friend, and when he asked me to marry him, I thought to myself that if the marriage did not work it would be terrible for both of us. He was also divorced; I think his wife had remarried.

I wrote to my brothers, because I asked them everything. I also consulted my son, because I was a widow and was supposed to obey my son.

Fourth Brother wrote from Australia, "Let me think it over."

Second Brother, too, could not make up his mind whether I should marry again. One day I would get a telegram that said, "Yes," the next day a telegram that said, "No." My brothers loved me so much; they did not want to see me hurt again. Also, there is the Chinese thinking that a widowed woman should not marry again because it brings dishonor to the family. But Hsü Chih-mo and I had already been divorced before his death. So I felt that I would not bring dishonor to the family if I married again.

Second Brother, who always told me to look inside myself, wrote:

> Your brother is not talented. You have been a widow for the past
> thirty years, educating your son by the lamp, and I was never
> able to give you any help. Now, I am old . . . your remarriage is a
> matter of reputation and propriety. I cannot put in one word. My

dear sister, you are a wise woman. You should make your own decision.

And A-huan, my son, responded:

My dear mother, you have been living in widowhood for some thirty years. You gave me life and affection; you nourished me, brought me up. The favor you have bestowed on me is as vast as the wide sky. Fortunately, I am independent and self-sufficient now. . . . I will continue to obey your wishes and follow your path of life. I will strive to make my life worthy of your favors. . . .

In past days you suffered too much. Mother, you have had little happiness. Your duty as a mother is fulfilled, and now your heart should be comforted. Who will comfort you? Who will keep you company? If you have found the right person, Mother, I will serve him as though he were my real father. . . .

My son had entered the profession of civil engineer when he moved to America. But when he wrote that letter to me, everyone who read it said that it showed he was Hsü Chih-mo's son.

Fourth Brother never replied. But, because my son gave permission, and Second Brother did not object, I married Dr. Su. Did I love him? Even that I cannot say. When I married him, I thought, Will I be able to do anything for this man? Will I be able to help him become a success?

When we first got married, every night after dinner his son and three daughters would leave the table very quickly and I always wondered why. They told me that their father quarreled with them after he had had a few beers or some wine. So they wanted to leave the table before he lost his temper.

When I told Dr. Su this, he was surprised. He did not know it himself. I said to him, "How about you stop drinking? Then the children will stay."

So from that day forth he stopped forever. Never another drop. This I very much admired about him, to have a habit like that and then be able to stop. After that, the children stayed on at the table.

With Dr. Su, I could have a conversation, discuss things with him. I could also help him. When he first moved to Hong Kong and had to get his license to practice, I stayed up with him all night as he read his thick medical books. Later he had two offices, one across the harbor in Kowloon during the morning, and another in Hong Kong. I kept track of all the books and appointments for him. If someone called with an emergency, I would meet him with the car at the Star Ferry Station, and tell him where to go next.

In 1967, I even went with Dr. Su back to Cambridge, Berlin, all the places from my past. He had lived in Japan most of his life and never journeyed west. I showed it to him. He and I sat on the banks of the Cam watching the river as it wound by the colleges. And I realized how beautiful Cambridge was; I had never known that before. We even took a bus from Cambridge to Sawston, and I just stood outside the cottage, staring. I could not believe I was so young then.

When we went to Berlin, the whole city was different. So many of the areas had been bombed during World War II. And I could not even walk to the Brandenburg Gate or Unter den Linden, because it was directly behind the Berlin Wall. But I managed to stand outside one or two buildings and see my old homes with Peter and Dora.

After visiting these places, I decided it was important for the grandchildren to learn about Hsü Chih-mo. So I asked a scholar and former colleague of Hsü Chih-mo's on the *Crescent Moon Monthly*, Liang Shiqiu, to compile an anthology of all Hsü Chih-mo's works. I donated some of my letters, and A-huan went to Taiwan to meet with him. I wanted my son and grandchildren to have something to remember Hsü Chih-mo by.

Dr. Su died in 1972. Just like my son Peter, in Germany, Dr. Su was afflicted with trouble in the intestines, in his case cancer. One day I met him at the ferry, and he was perspiring right through his woolen jacket in the middle of June. The doctor said to me, "You have six months. You have to prepare." We buried him in Hong Kong.

After Dr. Su's death I came to America to be near my son and grandchildren. Now every morning I rise at seven-thirty and do forty-five minutes of calisthenics. Then I sit for breakfast, a bowl of oatmeal or an egg boiled for two and a half minutes. I always take my vitamins and a spoonful of brewer's yeast in orange juice to keep my health. I like to read my newspapers, visit with my family and even join some of the classes offered by my housing complex. I can take German, aerobics or crocheting, all for older people. I still play mah-jongg now every week, allowing myself about two hundred dollars of winnings or losings throughout the year.

You always ask me if I loved Hsü Chih-mo, and you know, I cannot answer this. It confuses me, this question, because everyone always tells me that I did so much for Hsü Chih-mo, I must have loved him. But that I cannot say, what is love. In my entire life I have never said to anyone, "I love you." If caring for Hsü Chih-mo and his family was love, then maybe I loved him. Maybe, out of all the women in his life, I loved him the most.

EPILOGUE

I saw Yu-i on what was to be her last evening, January 20, 1989. She was still at home, but in bed most of the time, suffering from bronchitis. Her granddaughter Angela cared for her tirelessly. It was Angela's birthday and I stayed with Yu-i so Angela could go out to dinner with her husband and son.

The year before, I had dreamed Yu-i's death, a nightmare of her choking and gasping for air as she shrank in size on the edge of the bed. But, seeing her now, weak and shrunken, stunned me. I remembered the fierce look she used to get in her eyes when we talked; now they were filled with fluid. As she dabbed continually at her eyes with tissue, I could not tell if she was crying or suffering from a symptom of her illness. She coughed frequently, too, stirring up a tremendous amount of phlegm with each convulsion.

Sitting together at the teak table where we always had our interviews, I dwarfed her. She had very little appetite and ate only half a bowl of rice. It also took great effort for her to swallow her pills; I had to place them on her tongue and hold the glass of water to her lips. At one point, during the meal, she choked on a kernel of rice, and it was so scary, so real, a sound right out of my dream. The spasm took so much strength out of her, I feared she was going to die right there at the table.

The rest of the meal felt like a sad reminder of our times together. I washed the dishes as she sat there listlessly, then, with a walker, led her to the bathroom and finally to bed. She could no longer undress herself without great difficulty, and I slowly helped her into her pajamas, as she conscientiously made an effort to lift her arms and legs to assist. Buttoning her pajama top as she sat on the bed, I sensed in her a tremendous exhaustion, a complete yielding.

When I carefully shifted her body to pull back the covers and help her into bed, she took my hand and said to me hoarsely, but with more strength than I had heard her speak with that night, "I am so glad that you are here, you know."

I nodded in return, then kissed her good night. I made myself comfortable on the couch on the other side of her studio apartment and listened to her deep, labored breaths as she drifted for the final time into sleep.

The funeral was held at the Brick Church on Ninety-first Street and Park Avenue a few days later. I was astonished at the number of people who showed up, about two hundred. I spotted family, and familiar faces from the apartment building, her neighbors with whom she shared food and practiced German. Angela, who had always been close to Yu-i, pointed out others: Yu-i's mah-jongg friends and congregation members. The air was solemn but spirited, as if everyone present was aware of the long and prosperous life Yu-i had lived.

Angela's husband rose to speak and expressed admiration for Yu-i's energy and *nenggan* (can-do) spirit. I saw faces light up with recognition. This was the person most people knew, an open, determined woman, a teacher in the community. Angela also asked me to say something. I heard my voice reverberate around the room as I leaned into the microphone. I told of my years with Yu-i, how I had first read about her in a footnote while studying Chinese history in college. While still a student, I began to visit with Yu-i and asked her to tell me her story.

Standing in front of all who had gathered, I shared with them Yu-i's little-known past, how she had been married once to Hsü Chih-mo, suffered a divorce and emerged a strong woman with both traditional and modern values. From the reaction of those assembled, I could tell that few of them had known of Yu-i's association with Hsü Chih-mo, of her struggle for independence, selfhood. Watching those around me, I recognized that Yu-i had given something different to each person. And it was then I realized the great gift she had given me.

Kneeling in front of the mahogany trunk at my parents' house, I hold close Yu-i's black silk dress, her cheongsam, as if the garment itself might summon forth my great-aunt. A pattern of lotus flowers is woven into the smooth fabric, creating the effect of a shimmering black pond. Yu-i said she liked this textured material because it wore well and hid creases. She also modified her dress from the traditional narrow cheongsam by eliminating some darts and opening the side seams to allow for more movement. Regarding the distinctive lines of Yu-i's custom-made cheongsam, I remembered with appreciation her practicality and independence.

I have come now to place two articles of clothing in the trunk alongside Yu-i's. My two wedding dresses. The first, a gown of white chiffon—the stuff of my American childhood fantasies—I wore as I pronounced my marriage vows. The second dress, a full-length silk sheath in bright red, the Chinese color for felicity. Slim, slitted and topped with a stiff, stand-up collar, my cheongsam is modeled after those worn by Yu-i and my mother. When I changed into my cheongsam for my wedding reception, I felt vibrant and proud, at once a filial daughter and self-reliant sister, though I had broken with tradition and married, with my parents' blessings, outside of my heritage.

Lingering in front of the trunk, I imagined for a moment Yu-i beside me. I carefully folded my white dress, my red cheongsam and Yu-i's black cheongsam together. I smoothed the layers of tissue paper between them. Then I placed the dresses alongside each other and quietly closed my family's chest of remembrances.

ACKNOWLEDGMENTS

I am grateful to many people.

First, the Hsü family, particularly Yu-i's beloved son and grand-daughter, Hsü Chi-kai and Angela, for allowing me to spend so many hours with Yu-i and pay tribute to her through this labor. I appreciate their sharing with me the family's precious photograph album and memories about the woman who loved them so dearly.

The calligrapher Qianshen Bai created the calligraphy for the characters "Yu-i and Chih-mo" on the book jacket.

My research on Hsü Chih-mo and other members of the May Fourth generation was greatly fortified by the scholarship of Leo Ou-fan Lee, Julia Lin, Jiang Fucong, Liu Shiqing, Jonathan D. Spence and Cyril Birch. I am particularly indebted to Messrs. Lee, Spence and Birch for their translations of Hsü Chih-mo's and Liang Qichao's personal papers and essays. Jonathan Spence read my writings as a high school student and encouraged my interest in Yu-i's story throughout the years, providing invaluable suggestions. His sensitivity as a scholar, reader and friend are a continual inspiration to me.

Chi-hung Yim at Yale University assisted me in translating the following: Yu-i's memorial poem to Hsü Chih-mo, Hsü Chih-mo's elegy to his son and Chang Chia-sen's and Hsü Chi-kai's letters to Yu-i. He and Vivian Lu, also at Yale, meticulously read the whole manuscript and made many helpful comments which greatly improved *Bound Feet and Western Dress*.

The professors and teaching fellows of the East Asian departments at Harvard University gave their time and expertise, creating an atmosphere of open scholarship. Wei-ming Tu was an excellent thesis adviser. Rulan Pian offered her remembrances of Hsü Chih-mo and insights into the time period. Wilma Fairbank graciously shared with me her memories of Lin Huiyin.

As much as I am indebted to these scholars, I must maintain that any inaccuracies in this book are my own.

Frances Bennett, Carolyn Yordan and Alec Gold encouraged my early writings. The National Foundation for the Arts provided a grant at a much-needed time. Without the critical eye of my classmates at Columbia University and the Writer's Voice, and the guidance of my writing teachers, Patricia Bosworth, Martha Golub and Alice Dark, this book could not have been written. Alice Dark, in particular, helped me bring the manuscript out to the world.

Lynne Goodwin and James Bulkeley provided invaluable suggestions. Charlotte Bacon, David Franklin, Judy Neugroschl and Ashar Qureshi suffered through countless drafts. Elizabeth Miles and Kate Young were my critics in Moscow. Samba, Calypso, Fred and Zoe never read *Bound Feet*, but they kept me grounded during its writing. So many of my friends believed in me and helped me during this long process. I am ever appreciative.

At Doubleday, past and present, I'd like to thank my first editor, Renée Zuckerbrot, who left before *Bound Feet and Western Dress* was completed but whose passion for the book and friendship I value enormously. My deepest gratitude goes to my editor, Betsy Lerner, who graciously stepped in and brought the project to its conclusion. I value not only her patience and good humor but her insightful comments and exacting eye. Her legendary editorial skills transformed this manuscript into a book. Many thanks also go to her assistant and my E-mail correspondent, Brandon Saltz. I am grateful to Ellen Sinkinson; Ellen Archer for her unwavering enthusiasm and creativity; and Jayne Schorn for an innovative marketing campaign. Many thanks to the marketing, sales and telemarketing departments for their early support. Kudos to Mario Pulice for a splendid jacket and Jennifer Ann Daddio for an elegant book design. Kacy Tebbel and the Doubleday copyediting staff made me mind my *p*'s and *q*'s. I also thank Martha Levin for supporting the project from the start.

I am deeply indebted to my extraordinary agent and friend Nicole Aragi, for her humor, grace and counsel. Her integrity and wisdom are unfailing; every writer should be as fortunate. I also thank Nicole's assistant at the Watkins-Loomis Agency, Lily Oei.

I am grateful to the members of the Chang and Pu family, who have shown me, more than anyone else, what it means to be a family and what it means to be Chinese. Before his death, my maternal grandfather, Hung-ki Pu, a talented linguist, was a great source of knowledge and inspiration. My parents sustained me through many difficult years, never wavering in their support of me and this project. They always let me find my own way, and their faith ensures I do not stray too far off the path. My husband, Dan, offered me a writing fellowship in Moscow, and continually teaches me about love and companionship.

Finally, I owe so much to Yu-i, who never failed in her patience with me and in her eagerness and ability to satisfy my curiosity. I shall never find the words to thank you, Yu-i.

ABOUT THE AUTHOR

Pang-Mei Natasha Chang was raised in Connecticut. She received her B.A. in Chinese Studies from Harvard and a J.D. degree from Columbia University School of Law. She practiced law in New York City before moving to Moscow, where she currently resides with her husband. *Bound Feet and Western Dress* is her first book.

RED CHINA BLUES
by Jan Wong

Jan Wong, a Canadian of Chinese descent, went to China as a starry-eyed Maoist in 1972 at the height of the Cultural Revolution. In the name of the Revolution, she renounced rock and roll, hauled pig manure in the paddy fields, and turned in a fellow student who sought her help in getting to the United States. She also met and married the only American draft dodger from the Vietnam War to seek asylum in China.

Red China Blues is Wong's startling – and ironic – memoir of her rocky six-year romance with Maoism that began to sour as she became aware of the harsh realities of Chinese communism and led to her eventual repatriation to the West. Returning to China in the late eighties as a journalist, she covered both the brutal Tiananmen Square crackdown and the tumultuous era of capitalist reforms under Deng Xiaoping. In a frank, captivating and deeply personal narrative, she relates the horrors that led to her disillusionment with the 'worker's paradise'. And through the stories of the people, Wong creates an extraordinary portrait of the world's most populous nation.

'With her unique perspective, Jan Wong has given us front row seats at Mao's theater of the absurd. It is hard not to laugh and cry . . . This book will become a classic, a must-read for anyone interested in China' *New York Times*

A Bantam Paperback

0 553 50545 9

A SELECTION OF NON-FICTION TITLES

THE PRICES SHOWN BELOW WERE CORRECT AT THE TIME OF GOING TO PRESS. HOWEVER TRANSWORLD PUBLISHERS RESERVE THE RIGHT TO SHOW NEW RETAIL PRICES ON COVERS WHICH MAY DIFFER FROM THOSE PREVIOUSLY ADVERTISED IN THE TEXT OR ELSEWHERE.

☐ 99600 9 **NOTES FROM A SMALL ISLAND** *Bill Bryson* £6.99
☐ 99690 4 **TOUCH THE DRAGON** *Karen Connelly* £6.99
☐ 99707 2 **ONE ROOM IN A CASTLE** *Karen Connelly* £6.99
☐ 14239 5 **MY FEUDAL LORD** *Tehmina Durrani* £5.99
☐ 14474 6 **IN BED WITH AN ELEPHANT** *Ludovic Kennedy* £6.99
☐ 13928 9 **DAUGHTER OF PERSIA** *Sattareh Farman Farmaian* £5.99
☐ 50552 1 **SPARRING WITH CHARLIE** *Christopher Hunt* £6.99
☐ 14544 0 **FAMILY LIFE** *Elisabeth Luard* £6.99
☐ 13356 6 **NOT WITHOUT MY DAUGHTER** *Betty Mahmoody* £5.99
☐ 40936 0 **THE HIDDEN CHILDREN** *Jane Marks* £5.99
☐ 40814 3 **THE HAREM WITHIN** *Fatima Mernissi* £6.99
☐ 14288 3 **BRIDGE ACROSS MY SORROWS** *Christina Noble* £5.99
☐ 14322 7 **THE MAZE** *Lucy Rhees* £6.99
☐ 40570 5 **PRINCESS** *Jean Sasson* £5.99
☐ 40805 4 **DAUGHTERS OF ARABIA** *Jean Sasson* £4.99
☐ 99749 8 **PORTOFINO** *Frank Schaeffer* £6.99
☐ 14252 X **LORDS OF THE RIM** *Sterling Seagrave* £6.99
☐ 14108 9 **THE SOONG DYNASTY** *Sterling Seagrave* £7.99
☐ 99658 0 **THE BOTTLEBRUSH TREE** *Hugh Seymour-Davies* £6.99
☐ 40886 0 **THE RAINBOW PEOPLE OF GOD** *Archbishop Desmond Tutu* £5.99
☐ 50545 9 **RED CHINA BLUES** *Jan Wong* £6.99

All Transworld titles are available by post from:

Book Service By Post, P.O. Box 29, Douglas, Isle of Man IM99 1BQ

Credit cards accepted. Please telephone 01624 675137,
fax 01624 670923, Internet http://www.bookpost.co.uk or
e-mail: bookshop@enterprise.net for details.

Free postage and packing in the UK. Overseas customers allow
£1 per book (paperbacks) and £3 per book (hardbacks).

Critical Acclaim for
BOUND FEET & WESTERN DRESS

'A touching, bittersweet evocation of China . . . A bright and welcome addition to the rich family memoir genre . . . A fascinating book . . . Mesmerizing, reminiscent of the novels of Ba Jin . . . Ms Chang [tells] her story with unassuming delicacy [and] has helped us all recover a rare, precious, painful moment in the great panoply of human predicaments'
New York Times

'This is a moving story very rooted in time and place and propelled by one woman's profound courage'
New York Daily News

'[A] rich, evocative memoir . . . [Chang] is most touching when describing her great-aunt's lingering conflicts and confusion . . . Little did [Yu-i] know that in her struggles to reconcile East and West, familial duty and personal desire, Yu-i left her great-niece a legacy about the struggle for self'
People

'A gripping, candid, dual memoir'
South China Morning Post

'As she movingly tells her great-aunt's story, Pang-Mei shares her own ideas and conflicts about being Chinese-American; by the book's end she is a lot wiser, and so are we'
Mademoiselle

'Chang Yu-i's story, an uplifting tale of cultural clash, heartbreak, dignity and, most important, self-discovery . . . lyrically demonstrates the power of conviction, the necessity of individual strength. It is a book of dreams and devastation, respect and revulsion. Chang has successfully and admirably crafted pain into beauty. *Bound Feet & Western Dress* is a triumphant read, an uplifting testament to human endurance'
World Journal

'The story of Chang Yu-i's life leads us straight to the heart of what it has meant for Chinese women in this century to try to be modern. Her experiences show vividly how for her one side of modernity was humiliation, heartache, and hardship. But under the persistent and thoughtful questioning of her great-niece, Chang Yu-i also reveals much more. The result is a book full of surprises, utterly different from the Chinese family sagas that have appeared in the last few years'
Jonathan Spence, author of *The Search for Modern China*